INTRODUCTION

DID YOU SAY WALLONIA ?

Does the name Wallonia mean anything to you ? To many of the French, it's a region further north than their own Département du Nord. Probably lost in a thick mist broken up by no more than a few grey spots. To the Dutch, it's the region "full of minor mountains". Others ask whether it is the part of Belgium that is French-speaking ! A rather short portrait of a region that deserves much better treatment... The name itself is only just over a century old. And this single concept is scarcely adequate to encompass a moral, cultural, political and economic entity that lacks a single identical history to cement it together. This is the thorny question of identity, which has long been the subject of a still inconclusive debate.

AN IDENTIKIT PICTURE

Wallonia is partly, but by no means exclusively, the Ardenne or Ardennes. It is difficult to decide whether to use singular or plural to describe a multifaceted region that is difficult to define, a region that is too fond of its liberty and independence to allow its countless charms to be ensnared in words.

The region lies at the very heart of Europe ; it is the natural extension of Brussels, the French-speaking big brother, the town that stands at its very gateway. Ardennes, along with the "Roman country" of Brabant and Hainaut, make up Wallonia, the Belgian South. There are somewhat more than three million Walloons, occupying slightly over one-half the territory of Belgium. It is a roughly triangular region covering a distance of no more than 87 miles from north to south and 120 miles from west to east. Almost 5800 square miles in all. Its provinces are the Walloon Brabant, Hainaut, Liège, Luxemburg and Namur. The Ardennes includes the Condroz, the Sambre-et-Meuse dip, Lorraine and the Plateaux - this is the everyday environment of its people.

Today the region's frontiers border France, the Netherlands,

3

Water-skiing on the R.Meuse.

West Germany and the Grandy Duchy of Luxemburg, with which it is on good terms.

Generally speaking, it is true to say that Wallonia is part of the tectonic structure formed by the French Ardennes and the German and Luxemburg Eifel ranges. Yet it is different because it contains a quick succession of natural features that may be modest in size but that are unusually varied. Nevertheless, there is nothing agressive about this gentle landscape broken up by horizontal lines.

Water may be one of its main resources, but it is also one of Wallonia's traits of character, and everything revolves around the rivers Sambre and Meuse.

Especially the Meuse - a veritable hyphen, a way forward, a truly European river providing, as if contemporary history had not given reminders enough, a wonderful strategic line shadowing that of the Rhine. It is a geographical, economic and cultural turntable, the point at which various currents in civilisation converge. Wallonia has often played a major role in History. From Tournai, the earliest capital of the Western world, to Godefroi de Bouillon, the first King of Jerusalem; from Waterloo where the foundations of modern Europe were laid to Bastogne and the Battle of the Ardennes, a decisive spot in the destiny of a world at war. It is, then, hardly surprising that History and Art have left some of their richest marks in the stone of the monuments, on the façades of the houses and through the treasures in the museums.

A sailing school in Butgenbach.

Guy Lemaire

Wonderful Wallonia

Translated by Angela Moyon

Top:
*Citadel and
collegiate church in Dinant.*

Middle: *The gardens in Annevoie.*

Bottom: *The keep in Crupet.*

Front cover: *Durbuy.*

Back cover:
Countryside in the Ardennes.

A REGION
FOR ALL SEASONS

Yet there is nothing stuffy and immovable about this region and it cannot be talked about in the past tense. Wallonia is a pleasant place to visit because its surprises are carefully prepared and distilled a few at a time. This is the place to experience the little things in life that make for real enjoyment. At any time of the year, what's more - and that is what makes it so charming and attractive despite the fact that it is not what one might call a "born" tourist area. A place to visit in any season of the year ? There is the blossom of springtime in the town centres, the water and sports facilities in summer, the long walks in the depths of autumn and the frosty sparkle of winter that makes the region look like "a landscape from Grimm's fairytales" to use Hemingway's expression !

The region is also a balanced blend of beautiful towns and green countryside, dense forests and gently-rolling hills. There is fertile land and pleasant areas of wood and thicket ; the remains of man's industry and the elegant castles of the lords of a bygone age. If boredom really is born on a day of total uniformity, it is hardly surprising that the feeling is unknown here !

And while you revive flagging spirits, you can also improve your health. The air is still unpolluted and the climate, despite a very unfair reputation, is of the temperate maritime type, devoid of any extremes. One of the most invigorating anywhere in Europe ! Springs provide a real tonic. And "taking the waters" is, after all, just another form of tourism. It was not by chance that the English word "spa" originated from the name of a Belgian town. But this is just one attraction !

Château de Belœil.

There are a hundred others ready and waiting to appeal to your senses - grottoes, abbeys, leisure parks, sports centres, tourist trains, boats, cable cars. The choice is yours !

For those who prefer activity-packed holidays, there is plenty of opportunity in Wallonia to burn up excess energy. Skiing in winter (there are some sixty skiing days per year), climbing, boating, cycling, pony trekking, golf (a sport that is undergoing rapid expansion at the present time), sports grounds in every town, windsurfing, good fishing, and walking - enough to fill a lifetime !

CATERING
FOR THE INNER MAN -
AND WOMAN !

Just what it takes to give you an appetite ! Getting to know a country involves discovering its food as well, after all. Here the art of cooking and the intense pleasure of enjoying food has been raised to a fine art. Our gas-

5

Good food from Wallonia.

they are celebrated with the same fervour. There are the frenzied days of the Shrovetide Carnival when entire communities fall into a trance, for example to the rhythm of the Gilles' clogs ringing out on the cobblestones of Binche. There are the bonfires that chase away evil spirits and winter, all at the same time. There are the giants and their ungainly dances in the Ducasses. There are the proud walkers of Entre-Sambre-et-Meuse, their backs bent below the weight of uniforms dating back to the days of the Empire.

And last but not least, there are the village fêtes, popular events that enthusiasts are attempting to maintain in their strictly original form.

Nothing sad about all that, unlike the legends that are rife in the region and that are still recounted to the present day, with a twinkle in the eye, while the storyteller pretends to believe every word... This permanent party is waiting for you.

Another means of enjoyment is provided by the dozens of repertory and experimental theatres that fill rural life and evenings in town alike. The orchestras have created a flattering reputation for themselves for which the lyric theatre is also a strong contender.

tronomic delights are delightful examples of regional dishes, all of them healthy and plain, delicious and substantial. They have real taste. They are colourful. Family cooking with no need for hors d'oeuvres, main courses simmered slowly and watched over by grandmothers. Dishes with a touch of genius created by master chefs. Local chocolate is almost sinful! Beer and cheeses are still known by a wide variety of names that conjure up visions of rural life at its best and are always surprising. Hams, salt pork dishes, and the solid country loaves made with spelt and rye are sure to satisfy even the largest of appetites.

Often the dishes are linked to annual festivities. And they are not in short supply! Most of them represent traditions that have come down through the centuries and have resisted changes in fashion. Proof indeed that they are an integral part of the popular character. Whether profane (if not utterly pagan) or religious,

The carnival in Stavelot.

Festivals bring audiences flocking to theatres and concert halls in the winter and to streets and parks in the summer.

Are we not, after all, in the land of Georges Simenon, Magritte and Delvaux, Grétry and César Franck ? And why not ask Tintin, Spirou or the Smurfs to guide you on your way ? They will tell you exultantly that, among a thousand other historical facts, their ancestors created the Paris Metro, the tramways of Cairo, the iron foundries of Sweden, and the mining industry in the Soviet Union, and that they were the co-founders of New York and the pioneers of German industry. Let's stop there, in case the cockerel that is Wallonia's emblem chokes itself with pride !

So now you know ! All that remains is for you to discover the rest for yourself. And that's quite a task ! Take your time about it. Your holidays or long weekends.

The famous wall of rock in Freyr.

The zoo in Han-sur-Lesse.

Accommodation in Wallonia will cater for your wishes and suit your pocket. Modern hotels, or the more rural charms of country inns. Self-catering in flats, chalets, or villas, campsites deep in the heart of the country, hostels for the younger members of the family and B&B in farmhouses, which is always a rewarding experience for town-dwellers. The tourist offices and central booking agencies will organise a programme of visits to suit you personally… And how about a little memento of your stay ? Take a little bit of our region back home with you in the shape of items made by local craftsmen in wood, pewter, crystal, copper, or iron. There isn't a single raw material that our craftsmen don't know how to use, because strict rules govern the passing on of the

purest forms of specialist knowledge and the craftsmen work in the noblest of natural materials.

Wallonia. Ardennes. A multi-faceted land, we said. A puzzle, a miniature Europe that you are sure to enjoy assembling. The warm welcome is already there. You know the address. It's never far away and the roads are good. The South of Belgium is a warm place to live !

The following pages give a mere outline of some of Wallonia's "tourist" attractions. We divided it roughly into six regions with more natural features in common than administrative divisions. You won't find extensive detail but the signposts are there, ready to take you along routes of discovery.

Enjoy your read - and enjoy your trip !

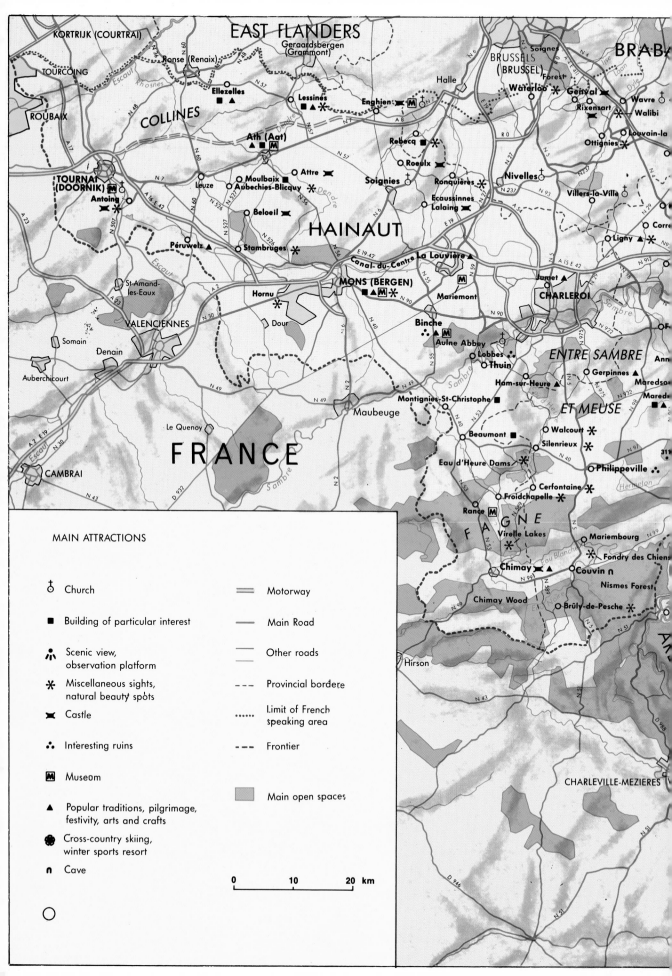

MAIN ATTRACTIONS

☥ Church

■ Building of particular interest

🐾 Scenic view,
   observation platform

✳ Miscellaneous sights,
   natural beauty spots

🛡 Castle

∴ Interesting ruins

Ⓜ Museum

▲ Popular traditions, pilgrimage,
   festivity, arts and crafts

❀ Cross-country skiing,
   winter sports resort

ᴖ Cave

═══ Motorway

─── Main Road

─── Other roads

- - - Provincial border

····· Limit of French
      speaking area

– – – Frontier

▮ Main open spaces

0   10   20 km

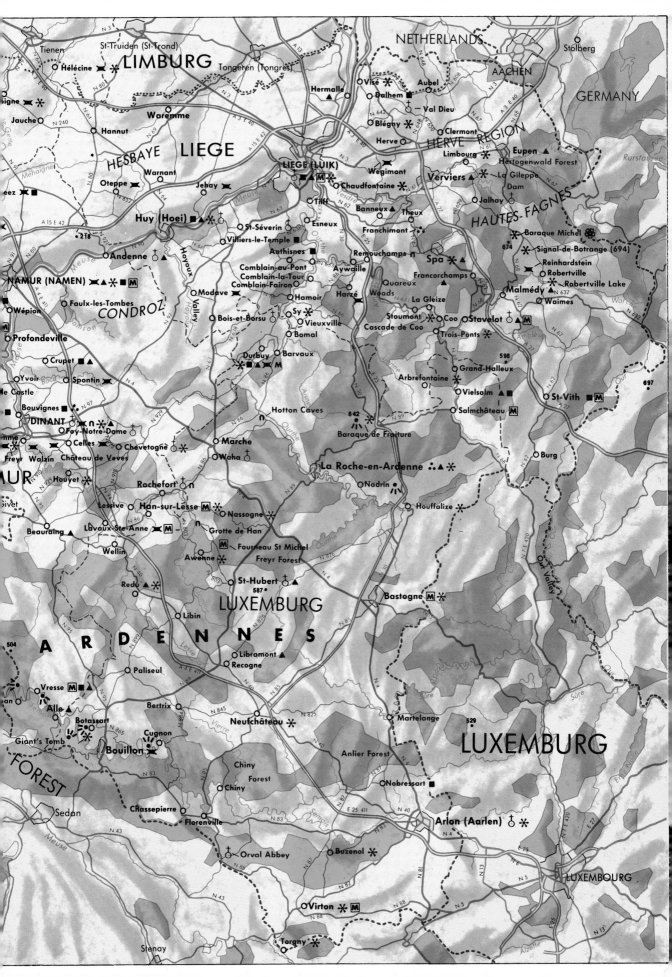

THE HILLS OF TOURNAI AND MONS

A white and grey landscape, and green countryside - subtle pastel colours abound here, blending softly with the local stone. This is Hainaut, "the God-given and sun-drenched land". Tournai and its cathedral, Beloeil and its castle, and the town of Mons all stand out like lighthouses without completely putting in the shade (although they do overshadow them somewhat) the other "lesser marvels" that require slow painstaking discovery and remain hidden to tourists in a hurry !

Tournai, which was French for many a long year, was also the capital of the Western world when the Frankish kingdom was ruled by Childeric. Like Tongres (and Arlon), it claims the title of "Belgium's oldest town". But what use are superlatives in describing its cathedral ? It is simply the largest one in the country and one of the most important in the history of the Western world. The towers (the famous "five bell-towers"), its massive nave (436 ft. long and 215 ft. wide), and the richness of its architecture (which is symbolic of mediaeval buildings) all emphasise its perfection. The main points of interest are the transept, the "cathedral within a cathedral", the Gothic chancel that contrasts starkly with the Romanesque nave, and the Renaissance pulpit. But the stained glass windows, carvings and treasure (Notre-Dame and St. Eleuthere reliquaries) are just as wonderful. The most interesting view of this masterpiece can be had from the Place Emile-Janson.

The chancel in Tournai Cathedral.

Tournai - the cathedral with the five towers.

Yet it is not the only place worth seeing in a town whose centre was badly bombed during 1940. Patient rebuilding (or more exactly "restoration") gave it back all its glory as well as its soul. The finest example of this is the main square on which stands the oldest belltower in Belgium. There are other sights too, like the Romanesque houses in the Rue Barre-Saint-Brice. The R.Schelde (Escaut) flows peacefully through Tournai and the town can be seen from the river (organised boat trips). Boats pass beneath the Bridge of Holes (Pont des Trous) where the fortifications date from the 13th century.

The lively bustling town of Tournai has always been a major cultural centre as is shown by its museums - Natural History, Arms and Weaponry, History and Archaeology (housing a collection of tapestries woven in Tournai) and most importantly the Art Gallery. A Horta building houses some of the most beautiful of all Manet's works, with a number of paintings by Seurat and Monet. The Folklore Museum, housed in a typical

11

Roodscreen in Tournai Cathedral.

17th-century house with a double gable and arches on the upper storey, illustrates local lifestyles and traditions. And the traditions are still very much alive. There is, for example, the procession to Our Lady of the Sick (Notre-Dame des Malades) on the nearest Sunday to the 8th September ; or the Four-Procession Festival in June ; or again the Flower Market on Good Friday and the Lost or Perjured Monday that follows Epiphany. Ample opportunity to try Monarchs' Rabbit with the delicious Tournai mixed salad, followed (why not ?) by plum tart or by "faluches", cakes made with butter and brown sugar. Not forgetting the "ballons noirs" (black balls) that are so hard to bite !

into a Belgian area and a French area. A Ribbon Museum serves as a reminder of the traditional regional industry. **Wervicq** still has some small-scale tobacco production. **Ploegsteert**, which has an English memorial and cemetery, bears witness to the bitter struggles of the "Great War".

If you skirt the French border and "flirt" with Flanders, you will come back to **Mouscron**, a major textile town. A few interesting sights, a large number of shops, the Léon-Maes Folklore Museum (with reconstitutions of 19th-century workshops), the former Count's Castle, and a vast central park will all make your stop enjoyable. In the first weekend in October, Mouscron celebrates the Hurlus (or "huleurs"), the nickname given to the Protestant footsoldiers - who are thrown down to the crowd from the top of a revolving ladder.

Estaimbourg has pleasure gardens with a fish-filled lake reflecting the walls of the castle built by Charles of Burgundy. Some of the 74 rooms are used for temporary exhibitions. Half-a-mile away is the strange **Mont-de-l'Enclus**, a happy example of linguistic cohabitation ! The north-facing slope is Flemish ; its south-facing slopes in Hainaut are covered with woodland and footpaths, inns and restaurants. In short, a small rural holiday resort with an observation platform from which, in fine weather, you can see more than one hundred towers and belltowers in the surrounding countryside. But don't worry, there's an orientation table to help you get your bearings !

Let's pass from one hill to another, **Mont-Saint-Aubert**, which is still known as Trinity Hill, is all of 478 ft. high ! It is a geological station, a holiday resort, and a hillside (with very well-developed hotel and leisure amenities) which inspired many a poet. Some of

them lie buried here in the "Poet's Garden" created in 1971 around a church that is also a place of pilgrimage. Every year, on Whit Saturday, there is a "Poets' Feast". The participants process up the cobbled path known as the Poets' Path. It may be paved with cobblestones but there is also poetry engraved in it.

Beyond Calonne (Château des Quatre-Vents visited by Louis XV) to the south of Tournai lies **Antoing** and the white country. Its nickname comes from the limestone quarries (there is a Stone Museum) and the lime kilns that once provided employment for the entire region. Charles de Gaulle, though a native of Lille, studied here for some time. A few natural features (including the so-called "Billemon Hole" tumulus) confirm the town's Gallo-Roman origins. The most interesting sight is the Ligne family castle where the initial peace talks were held prior to the end of the One Hundred Years' War. The Neo-Gothic construction still includes a few older sections, such as a tall 15th-century keep flanked by a turret built a century later. Once you have climbed the 275 steps to the top, and as a reward for your efforts, you will find a magnificent panoramic view.

As you will have guessed, you cannot get to know a town like Tournai properly in a couple of hours. Especially as its "outlying areas" are also worth a visit.

To the north and west, head for **Comines** which the R.Lys divides

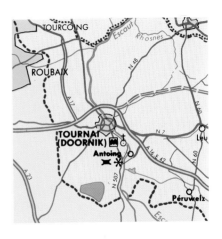

Château d'Antoing.

A Renaissance town hall and the former Cloth Hall complete the places of interest in this small town. Nearby, there is Bruyelle (18th-century castle and lake), **Peronnes'** "Grand Large", a vast 45-hectare lake in the heart of the forest used entirely for tourism, the impressive Hollain standing stone ("the stone that turns") and **Fontenoy**.

"Gentlemen of the English Army, please fire first". A famous sentence spoken here during a historic battle that, on 11th May 1745, opposed French troops under Maréchal de Saxe and the allied forces from England, the Netherlands, and Austria. The daring Irish soldiers, remembering the carnage in Limerick, helped the French to victory. A Celtic cross and a plaque in the cemetery wall serve as reminders of their courage. Warlike memories have little place in **Lesdain**, which is as well known for its nurseries and rose gardens as it is for its endless fields of strawberries that produce the appropriately-named "Reine" (Queen).

To the south-east of Tournai, the most interesting place is **Peruwelz**, a former wool town that is worth a stop. **Bonsecours** has been a well-known place of pilgrimage for the past 400 years. Its basilica was built around the tiny, miraculous Virgin Mary that once stood against the trunk of a tree in the old charcoal forest. An annual procession is held in honour of the statue, on the first Sunday in July. As a matter of interest, the walls of the Neo-Gothic basilica are only a foot away from the French border! The present 1,200-hectare State forest delights hikers and riders alike. As for the Forest Centre, which is open in the peak tourist season, it is a mine of interesting information. It also houses frequent exhibitions.

One of the most important discoveries ever made in Belgium dates from 1878 and it was made in **Bernissart**. A miner unearthed skeletons of iguanodons in the Fosse Sainte-Barbe. Today, they can be seen in the Museum of Natural Sciences in Brussels. A pleasant little museum covers this subject as well as other events in local history.

Blaton, which holds a Camlet Fair and an "All Saints" pilgrimage on the 1st November every year, has three canals flowing through it (water sports).

Harchies and its vicinity stand in vast marshes, the largest stretch of wetlands in Wallonia. They were formed by the compacting of the subsoil in mining galleries. Now a nature reserve that is open to the public (guided tours), they are a sort of birdwatchers' paradise. In the village, the Hussards Society traditionally decapitates an (already-dead) goose on the first Wednesday after the first Sunday in July.

Once you have crossed the Mons-Paris motorway, you will find yourself heading for the **Haut-Pays** (Uplands), brought to life by the two rivers Honnelles. This is a rolling, tranquil part of the Ardennes. The great poet Émile Verhaeren enjoyed going for long walks in **Caillou-qui-**

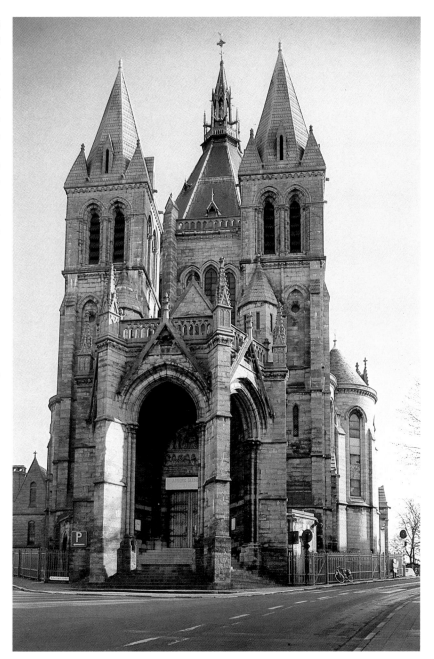

Basilica of Notre-Dame de Bonsecours.

Bique, where he lived and worked (his study is open to the public). The whole region abounds with tiny rustic villages (Angre, Marchipont, Montignies-sur-Roc etc.) and long walks. One of them, which is quite unique in its own special way, takes you past numerous old farm implements (in Honaelles). A veritable open air museum.

Before reaching the Borinage, the road will take you through Dour and its pottery workshops.

15

The Grand Hornu.

It is in the dour **Borinage,** an area of industrial development and workers' protests, that we find the **Grand Hornu,** an industrial site famous throughout Europe. In the early years of the 19th century (when there were 400 working-class homes), the factory and housing were integrated into the same monumental complex. A conservation group now organises numerous cultural events there. It was in the Borinage area that Vincent Van Gogh was, for some time, a pastor saving souls before going on to the South of France. He lived in Wasmes and Cuesmes where his room has been refurbished as it was then.

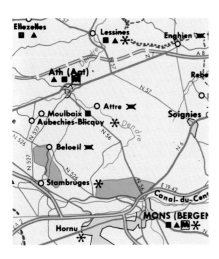

Mons, the old drapers', brewers' and merchants' town, is the county town of Hainaut. A provincial capital, if you prefer. It is one of Belgium's main arts centres. Urban renovation has had no effect on the old heart of the town, with its attractive squares and narrow, windy, cobbled streets that heave their way up the hill covered with bourgeois residences. This a cultural centre and university town with large numbers of busy shops, but it also cultivates a high sense of tradition. The most famous of all is the so-called Lumeçon, the fight between St. George and the Dragon, played out to the "Air of the Doudou" at Holy Trinity. Tens of thousands of spectators take part in it, as they do in the Golden Carriage Procession before tasting the splendours of the Ducasse.

The Golden Carriage, an impressive decorated coach, is housed in the collegiate church of Saint Waudru, built in the 15th century after being commissioned by the canonesses. The impressive building with its 29 chapels round about, is one of the best examples of Gothic architecture as it was understood in the Brabant. With the Baroque belltower (283 ft. high and with a merry peal of 47 bells) and the Town Hall, the

The belfry in Mons.

church is the third of the town's main monuments. On the front of the beautiful Town Hall is the popular statuette of a monkey in the "Grand Guard". If you do stop in Mons, don't forget to go and stroke his head - it ensures future happiness ! The Town Hall overlooks the Mayor's garden where you may be sprayed by the "Rapieur", a statue of a local street urchin. Some of Mons' museums stand in these gardens (numismatics, ceramics, prehistory, and the War Museum). But they are not the only museums in the town. The Jean-Lescarts Residence illustrates local life, while the Chanoine-Puissant Museum whose architecture is typical of 16th-century Mons houses the

The monkey of the "Main Guard".

the beer-based dishes that have become their speciality.

From Mons, an 'A' road (route nationale) runs to Soignies, through the forest where SHAPE (Supreme Headquarters of Allied Powers in Europe) had its h.q. during World War II.

Soignies grew up around an abbey founded c. 650 by (St.) Vincent. A 7-mile procession and a famous historical cortege honour the patron saint on Whit Monday. This is the region of the "Cayoteûs" (quarrymen from the small granite quarries), and Soignies has a collegiate church that is a wonderful example of the Early Romanesque style. In addition to its massive yet harmonious architecture, it houses a few masterpieces. The old cemetery nearby has been turned into a public park, with a chapel, shrines and Cross.

In the same area shaped by the rivers Senne, Sennette and Samme, lies **Enghien**, once the property of the Arenberg family. Its 17th-century park, which is open to the public, is one of the most remarkable anywhere in Europe (265 hectares). Lakes, a canal, a pavilion, stables, and a 13th-century chapel adjoining the castle all come into view as you stroll along. In town, St. Nicholas' Church and the Capuchins' Church are full of art and history. The Jonathas House is also worth a visit; it is an illuminating museum of ancient tapestry. From one quarry to another - here we are in Dendre and **Lessines** (René Magritte's birthplace).

At this point, we are entering the Hill Region that stretches along the border with Flanders. Lessines was the subject of many a dispute and it was damaged during numerous armed conflicts over the course of the centuries. It is one of these battles that is commemmorated during the Festin, a traditional colourful procession held on the first Saturday in September. Another traditional procession, but this time of a religious nature, is the Black Penitents' Procession (on the evening of Good Friday) which is said to date from the 15th century. It takes place to the dull, throbbing beat of drums. The most interesting building in Lessines is Our Lady of the Rose Hospital (so-called after its founder's coat-of-arms). The abbey buildings, which were rebuilt in the 17th century, house several fine art collections.

Once you arrive in the **Hill Region** (Région des Collines), you are in the very heart of verdant countryside. The rolling winding landscape has large villages perched at the top of short inclines. This is a region devoted to farming and stock-breeding but which has made great efforts to prove its worth to tourists. Around **La Hamaide**, for example, there is a living Museum based on a principle that is as simple as it is attractive. Craftsmen (farmers, a basket maker, an art metalworker) open the doors of their workshops to the public and invite you to "have a go" (there is also a Harness-Making Museum).

In **Ellezelles**, the Wild Cat Mill (Moulin du Cat Sauvage) is still in working order and still grinding corn. The environmental rangers in the Hill Region will be delighted to take you with them on their travels. But there are walks of a quite different type, too, on the "Bizarre Pathway", for example! Moreover, every summer (on

Enghien - the canal.

main works that once belonged to this collector. An Art Gallery and a Museum of Natural History complete the places to visit.

The Wauxhall Gardens and Grand Large Lake (near the motorway) are used as leisure areas. And whether you are a connoisseur or just very fond of food, the local people will be delighted to see you try their pork chops "à la Berdouille" and all

The Town Hall.

the last Saturday in June), witches assemble here for a feverish celebration of their sabbath... If you want to appear knowledgeable about their strange practices (they re-enact the executions of witches in the Middle Ages), you will have to start by learning their ritual slogan, ''Houp! Houp! Riki! Rikète! Padzeur les haies et les bouchons, vole au drâpe et co pus lon''...

In this close-knit region, it is obvious that there are still large numbers of merry traditions, all of them very much alive. This comes to the fore again in **Ath**, the walled town at the confluence of the two Dendres. During the fourth week in August, they celebrate the ''Giants' Ducasse''. Mr. and Mrs. Gouyasse (Goliath) are the legendary local giants who are as impressive for their height (they top 13 ft.) as for their weight (19 st). Samson, Miss Victory, the

Ath - the carnival and its Giants.▷

Ath Town Hall. ▽

Above : *The park at Beloeil.*

Opposite : *two rooms*
in the Château de Belœil.

Overleaf : *The Château de Beloeil*
in the midst of its superb parkland.

Four Aymon Boys, the Horse Bayard and other characters can all be seen in the Sunday procession. This is a golden opportunity for tasting the filling macaroon tart (tarte aux mastelles) - not to be confused with the creamy curd tart made in Lessines (tarte à maton) !

Visitors should be sure to see the Baroque Town Hall, St.Julian's Church (with its treasure trove of gold and silverware), St.Martin's Church (wayside cross), the Burbant Tower (12th-century keep), the old houses, and the portcullis bridge (the remains of Vauban's fortifications). And no visit would be complete without a trip to the museum to see the Mainvault ''Entombment of Christ'' (15th century).

In the Ath region, there is a lovely 18th-century country castle - **Attre**, which is worth a visit for its elegance and simplicity. In stark contrast, is the Belgian Versailles, **Beloeil**, which could be the subject of a book all by itself. Beloeil, the secular property of the family of the princes of Ligne, who still live in it, is always a dazzling sight - inside and outside alike (formal gardens, lakes, bowers, play area and miniature train). Tapestries, old masters, silverware, a library of 20,000 leather-bound books, unique items of furniture, and Chinese porcelain all bear profuse and magnificent witness to a family which has been present at all the great moments in Europe's history.

Countryside near Moulbaix.

The Marquise Mill in Moulbaix.

While you are in a region that encourages people to take their time, let yourself dawdle on to **Stambruges**. The sandy soil, arid wind, and scattered pine woods, moors and heather have won it the nickname "Sea of sand". In fact, it is a huge clearing where footpaths abound.

Tongre-Notre-Dame has a basilica built around a miraculous statue of the Virgin Mary which is honoured by a procession held on the fourth Sunday in September.

Moulbaix has the attractive "Marchioness's Mill" (1614). It is still in working order.

Chièvres (St.Martin's Church, leper hospice) and **Cambron-Casteau** (ruins of a Cistercian abbey) are yet more places to visit. As is the amazing Archeosite in **Aubechies**. This is an impressive open-air museum which, after many painstaking archaeological digs, shows visitors reconstructions of Gallo-Roman dwellings. A Roman villa (domus romana) is lived in permanently. Old crafts are brought to life on the site and every year there is a Gallic Festival that would do credit to Asterix himself!

The lilting names of three natural regions with borders as lightly-marked as three strokes of a pen. Yet they are peacefully encircled by the rivers Sambre and Meuse and the French frontier. Their "towns" are really little more than large villages, but their history is such that some of them justifiably boast of princely grandeur.

Thudinia, on the marches of Charleroi, is a large expanse of green countryside. There is something of the Ardennes about this region, with deep valleys, impressive rocks, a few happy "accidents" of nature, high plateaux and large forests.

Thuin stands in the heart of the region and of the valley that was once called the Valley of Science because of its numerous monasteries (more than twenty). On all sides, tributaries (the Blesmelle, Hantes, Thure, and Eau d'Heure) flow down to the Sambre that runs through Thuin itself. It's hardly surprising, then, that the town was once famous for its boatyards. And every year, this erstwhile population of mariners participates in nautical jousts as soon as summer returns. But the liveliest traditional event, here as everywhere else in the Entre-Sambre-et-Meuse area, is the "March" dedicated to St. Roch, which is held on the third Sunday in May.

The lower town in Thuin pays allegeance to the Sambre. A cobbled "wall" leads to the upper town. There is an interesting panoramic view from the top. The Notger Tower serves as a reminder of the fact that the town once belonged to the ancient Principality of Liège. The southern ramparts, which have recently undergone restoration, overlook hanging gardens. The belfry (1639) is all that remains of the old collegiate church. One of the streets is named after Maurice des Ombiaux, the writer who was the bard of both Thudinia and Burgundy. And his memorial statue in Thuin looks very like the one in Nuits-Saint-Georges. Another of the town's sights, and the symbol of local pride, stands at the end of the main street. It is the "Spantole" (Terrible), a bombard captured from the Prince of Condé's army after he had besieged the town for a fortnight. Just before reaching it, you will see the ancient almshouses of the Aulne and Lobbes abbeys that stand upstream and downstream of Thuin.

Aulne nestles close to the Sambre in gently-rolling luxuriou countryside. The ruins of it ancient abbey are impressive and among the finest in the country

The ruins of the former Aulne Abbey.

THE MARCHES OF ENTRE SAMBRE-ET-MEUSE

The Marches of Entre-Sambre--Meuse are undoubtedly one of e most spectacular traditional ents in Wallonia. With a very w exceptions, they are held in aces south of Charleroi, mainly the Hainaut province. Histo-ns and folklore specialists do ot all agree as to the origin of ese Marches (they date back to e 16th century) or to their func-on. Perhaps they are a reminder the rural militia that once flan-d sacred relics during proces-ons. The countryside was not a fe place in those days and an rmed escort was a necessity.

From May to September, some 'ty villages ''march''. To the und of drums, pipes and nds; to the sound of gunfire; the footsteps of sappers, gre-diers, light infantrymen and ouaves. Most of them on foot, e few officers on horseback. ot forgetting the canteen wor-rs who take care of the (gene-us) helpings of food (all well shed down). The marches are dicated in the main to St. Roch,

St. Rolende and St. Peter (and Paul). The best-known are held in Thuin and Ham-sur-Heure, Wal-court, Jumet (the oldest march, said to date back to 1380), Ger-pinnes (the longest - 22 miles) and Fosses-la-Ville where it is held only every seven years. The uni-forms are for the most part remi-

niscent of the days of Napoleon. The Marches in Entre-Sambre-et-Meuse, which usually take place over three days with the main event on the Sunday, involve more than five thousand partici-pants. Their social function is obvious, in addition to the tradi-tional colourful and poignant spectacle that they provide.

The Association of the Mar-ches in Entre-Sambre-et-Meuse can provide you with an annual calendar of events, most of them on fixed dates.

• Association des Marches folkloriques de l'Entre-Sambre-et-Meuse, c/o Lucien Sainthuile, rue Prince de Liège 25, 6280 Villers-Poterie/Gerpinnes.

There is a 16th-century Gothic church, a refectory, stables, a palace, and a farm that still has arcaded galleries and an inner courtyard. It is a place for meditation and surprises. In July, a major music festival is held there. Aulne is a place that visitors either pass through or stop in, a place where cafés and cruises on the Sambre abound. Further north, the Landelies marina underlines the importance of yachting on this river.

You can go to **Lobbes**, to the west of Thuin, by a local tramway that is much appreciated by tourists during the summer months. For eleven centuries, the abbey trained clerks who then worked throughout the Western world. All that remains of the abbey is the 18th-century portico, the Portelette. Nearby is the Carolingian church of St. Ursmer which towers over the surrounding countryside. The landscape is gentle, just right for pastoral walks to tranquil villages. There is Biercée, in cherry country, where every year on the second Sunday in July, a small-scale dis-

tillery produces the local brew. Or Hantes-Wihéries, with its countless shrines and its Stations of the Cross. Or Soire-sur-Sambre which has a remarkable moated fortress dating from the 13th and 14th centuries, an admirable reminder of mediaeval military architecture. Taken straight from a Romantic engraving comes the "Roman" bridge in Montignies-Saint-Christophe, just a stone's throw away from the frontier with France. Its thirteen arches span the pretty R. Hantes, forming a dam at the same time.

Beaumont has kept much of it character. It enjoys a privilegec position on an outcrop of rock high above the surroundin; plains. Within the one-and-a-hal miles of well-preserved town wal are countless winding alleyways some of them containing 16th century houses. The Salamande Tower now houses a folklore anc local history museum which inclu des references to the Holy Roma Emperor, Charles V. In 1549 three vagabonds from the Auver gne region of France met a noble man on horseback and forcec

The town walls in Beaumont

And now, get ready for the **Hainaut Boot**. A region of sylvan creatures and meadows, to quote an author. The "boot" is like a skilful piece of swordplay! A green sward where the villages look like pebbles strewn by Petit Poucet as he plays in the huge boot belonging to a peaceful ogre.

The localities are legion - Beaumont, Rance, Chimay, les Rièzes and les Sarts. This, then, is the Boot!

him to carry their heavy loads When they arrived in Beaumont the knight revealed his identity he was the Emperor, Charles V He had the three brigands arres ted immediately, which gave ris to a saying that is still in use : "Town of Beaumont, town o
　　　　　　　　　　[bad iuck
Arrived at noon, by one
　　　　　　　　　　[strung up.'
This unfortunate reputation il befits the pleasant character o

*An aerial view
of the Eau d'Heure Dam.*

*Water sports
on the Eau d'Heure lakes.* ▷

the local people. Perhaps their joviality comes from the traditional macaroons. The recipe was said to have been given to them by one of Napoleon's chefs who was billetted in Beaumont with the Emperor himself four days before the Battle of Waterloo.

South of Beaumont beyond Renlies (fortified church) and Vergnies (the birthplace of the French Revolution's favourite composer, François-Joseph Gossec), is an impressive beauty spot - the **Eau d'Heure Lakes**.

They will undoubtedly become a major tourist attraction in the near future.

The impressive dams (Eau d'Heure, Plate Taille, Féronval, Ry Jaune, Falemprise) were built

in the late 70's to regulate the flow of water from the R.Sambre. They are already used in part for water sports and are now part of a project to build an environmentally-integrated holiday resort.

The building programme includes hotels and service flats catering for 5,000 holidaymakers, an 18-hole golf course, a village providing shopping facilities and entertainment, a yachting marina, a multileisure complex, and walks - to be known as "**Port la Rochette**".

This does not mean that the nearby villages will lose anything of their original charm. Villages like Cerfontaine and its wonderful local history museum (housed in the former railway station), Froidchapelle, Boussu and its "little Switzerland", Roly (with its castle-farm), Thy-le-Château (mediaeval fortress), Senzeille (astronomical clock showing the main movements of the stars and their revolutions), and the largest of them all, **Walcourt**. It has a mediaeval layout (with one strange alleyway consisting of one long flight of steps) and it is particularly proud of St. Materne's Basilica which contains a statue of the Virgin Mary that was miraculously saved from an arson attack. The statue is carried round the village in procession every year at Holy Trinity, a "grand tour" lasting some 4½ miles. This is one of the most famous of all the so-called Entre-Sambre-et-Meuse marches. The basilica still has a very valuable "treasure".

Rance is a famous place and, although you might not know it, it stands in a wonderful setting of over 2,500 hectares of forest (and as many miles of footpaths, it seems), where a "red" marble used to be extracted. It was used to decorate altars of local churches (Barbençon) and to adorn the Hall of Mirrors in Versailles, the Rubens Room in the Louvre, the colonnades in St. Peter's in Rome, motifs in the Carthusian monastery in Pavia, and Napoleon's tomb in the Invalides! A museum flanked by an unusual marble library brings its history to life in an intelligent manner, and in several languages! It is not the only museum in the area. A Hunting Museum (the area is particularly well-stocked with game) has 2,000 stuffed animals on show. And in Sivry, the Nature

Boating on the Virelles Lake.

The elegant entrance to the Château de Chimay.

Museum (where more appropriate for this is right in the heart of nature) has a wide range of activities on offer for school parties.

As you go down towards Virelles, look for the Four Brothers' Tree, an oak with a trunk measuring 20 ft. in circumference at its base.

Virelles is one of the country's largest lakes (almost 120 hectares) and its waters ripple in the wind. Since 1983, it has been a nature reserve, although it has remained a major tourist attraction for family holidays. It is, in fact, a remarkable example of how nature conservancy (in particular the reed beds and nesting birds) can co-exist with tourism (guided tours, regatas, carriage rides, restaurants, Madame Tallien's pavilion, angling, beach, and play areas). It is one of the most unusual places in the region. The traditional dish here is "escavèche" fish (either trout or eel) prepared and preserved in vinegar with a variety of other ingredients. Pope John XXIII was extremely fond of it.

Ah, the sounds of **Chimay**! A town of princes and gastronomic temptation! It is bathed by the Eau Blanche. The chronicler Froissart was Canon-Treasurer of a collegiate church of immense richness, built of blue stone and slate, which contains the secret of the princes, locked away for ever in the white marble of their tomb. One of the vistas from the main square, which is as attractive as a theatre backcloth with its ring of old bourgeois houses, opens onto the castle. This was the ancestral home of the Princes of Croy then of Caraman-Chimay, and it is splendid for its well-balanced design. One cannot but admire the grey limestone and purple slate, the mullioned windows, the bulbous corner tower, the park with the great centuries-old trees.

Among its many treasures, you're sure to have a particular liking for the little theatre (a replica of the one in Fontaine-

33

bleau) dedicated to Madame Tallien, "Our Lady of Thermidor" who ended her days here after marrying the Prince. So many artists, at their head Liszt and La Malibran, performed here. Yes, this castle has a soul, no doubt about it ! Whether it is expressed in a violin played by Bériot or in the King of Rome's christening robe which is still kept here, in the floor of 46,000 slates or Louis XI's banners in the castle chapel. And the narrow cobbled streets that wind their way up to the castle add to the charm !

The "rièzes" are the vast marshes in an infertile plain. The "sarts" are the former stretches of forest in Thiérache that were gradually cleared over the years. The **Rièzes and Sarts Region** is well-suited to meditation. Was it, then, by mere chance that a community of Benedictines settled here in 1850 ? Today, Scourmont Abbey in Forges, "La Trappe", produces cheese and beer sold under the name of Chimay. With high exports, especially of beer, the products have gained a reputation for the entire area.

Although the Rièzes and Sarts Region (which has a lovely little museum in Cul-des-Sarts) was highly suitable for guerilla warfare, its layout and the proximity of France made it a smugglers' paradise. Most of the smuggling concerned tobacco, hence the common French expression, "Fume, c'est du belge !" ("Go on, smoke it, it's Belgian !"). The jovial wit of the local people is well-illustrated in the truculent popular character, Toine Culot, invented and narrated by the successful author, Arthur Masson.

High Command. The Viroin Reserve, a natural beauty spot that is as game-filled as the river is stocked with fish, extends beyond Dourbes, Olloy and Nismes. Geologically-interesting features abound. Like the Fondry des Chiens, a spectacular depression hollowed out as the limestone was slowly worn away by water.

The Reserve is the favourite haunt of botanists and is not well enough known by the general public (but perhaps it's just as well!). A small tourist train brings an added touch of enjoyment to these beauty spots; it runs through the Eau Blanche and Eau Noire Valleys which meet up in Nismes. The train takes you to **Couvin**, in the shadow of a limestone rock once topped by a castle that was razed to the ground on Louis XIV's orders. The small town is famous for its good food. In the centre (the starting point for many a walk) are the Cavernes de l'Abîme (Abyss Caves) in which there is an audiovisual presentation of Belgian prehistory. Nearby are the three-storey Neptune Caves (in Pétigny). This is where the Eau Noire disappears underground for $2\frac{1}{2}$ miles, cove-

ring the distance in 24 hours. Visitors can sail along the underground river in a boat and see a wonderful "son et lumière".

The villages along the road to Philippeville are few and far between. And who could argue with nature! You really must stop in Mariembourg (which gets its names from its founder, Mary of Hungary, the sister of Emperor Charles V).

The old fortress-town is built to a star-shaped layout with all its streets leading to a central square. Mariembourg draws the crowds because of the Three Valley Steam Railway. The excursion is particularly picturesque because the line follows all the meanders of the R. Viroin.

When Charles V was dislodged from Mariembourg by the King of France, he built Philippeville, named after his son, the future King of Spain. Here, too, the streets converge on the parade ground (Place d'Armes). Louis XIV's famous architect, Vauban, extended the fortifications here. The underground passages and an old powder magazine are open to the public. The road westwards takes you back to the Eau d'Heure Dams.

◁ *The little theatre in the Château de Chimay.*

The Three Valley Steam Train.

In an area once described as "the back of beyond" (because the main roads and rail links had all ignored it), progress if it exists at all has been unusually discreet. From days long gone, the area has kept its facetious, sensitive soul and a sort of natural reserve. Brought together by an unknown mysterious pact, the Fagne, the forests, and the valleys run one into another, all of them complementary. In Bruly-de-Pesche (open to visitors), Hitler sought shelter in his "Wolf's Lair" when plotting with the entire German

BRABANT - AND A PART OF HAINAUT

Take the whole of the Walloon Brabant and add a goodly measure of Hainaut and you will have erected a barricade in front of Brussels. A barricade which would be a natural barrier, a vegetable garden and a flower bed.

This is very fertile country, covered with farms, castles and abbeys that have been closely involved with History for centuries. But the apparent rural tranquillity soon changes, in the Central Region, into something harder and more obviously industrial. Because of this, traditional events are even more excessive, a just reward and a vital moment of forgetfulness for suffering humanity. It is said that the area between Wavre and Charleroi

and between Binche and Waterloo is rather more a place for quick but repeated excursions than a place to enjoy a long lazy holiday. But we'll leave it to you to judge for yourself...

Waterloo... Is the plain really as dreary as Victor Hugo described it plaintively ? 18th June 1815 tolled the death knell of a reign and an illusion ! But do you know that most of the battle took place in Placenoit, that Napoleon lodged in Vieux-Genappe (at the Ferme du Caillou) and that the "Lion" was erected on its mound in Braine-l'Alleud.. A long sign-

posted route will take you round the main stages in the fateful battle. Here and there are some fiteen monuments, farms and other strategic places which bring the Napoleonic disaster back to life.

In the high season, a small tourist train takes visitors to and from the centre of Waterloo itself, in fact a pretty, busy, little town that has a museum named

The Lion of Waterloo.

The inner courtyard in the Château de Rixensart.

after the victorious Duke of Wellington. Although for ever marked by this bloody episode in its history, the Romanic Country of Walloon Brabant is nevertheless a synonym for tranquil beauty whether you arrive from the west or from beyond the Six Valleys that cut into it on the eastern side. A 93-mile tourist road links one river to the other - Dyle, Petite-Gette, Grande-Gette, Lasne, Nethen and Train. It just shows how important water is in this rustic, bucolic countryside. In contrast to these fanciful rivers, **Genval**, the "pearl of the Brabant Ardennes" offers visitors the still waters of its lake. There are all the pleasant amenities that you might expect in such a remarkably graceful, rural environment of residential bungalows (with the luxurious Château du Lac as its centrepiece).

More impressive still is the Solvay estate in **La Hulpe**, on the edge of the Soignes Forest, a veritable forestry museum that is open to the public, unlike the adjacent castle.

In **Rixensart**, where there are vast stretches of woodland, the main attraction is the castle that belonged to the princely Mérode family. Based on Spanish Renaissance ideas, it overlooks formal gardens laid out in the style of Le Nôtre, and surprises visitors because of the soft pink tinges of its bricks while its rich furnishings, in particular its Gobelins tapestries, are sure to delight everybody.

Lasne is a fisherman's paradise. A hydraulic mill still works here; there is another one in **Couture-Saint-Germain**, within the abbey close. Here, as in Moustry and in the countless vil-

lages that we have visited, the church is worth a visit.

Spectacular, light as bubbles, the annual festival of hot air balloons in **Ceroux-Mousty** (held on Ascension Day, would you

believe !) is attended by an exceptionally large number of enthusiasts.

We then reach the town of **Ottignies** where the Bois des Rêves Estate is used entirely for tourism (walks, lakes, bird sanctuary, swimming pool, play area, lay-bys). But it is **Louvain-La-Neuve** that marks the region. This is the most recent town in Belgium, built between late 1960 and early 1970 to accommodate the impressive French-speaking section of the prestigious Louvain University - an astonishing "Campus-town in the country" (a footpath runs right through it) with, of course, the youngest population in Belgium and amenities such as a theatre, and a museum devoted to archaeology and the history of fine art.

Two views of Louvain-la-Neuve.

Wavre, the geographical heart of Belgium, is a leisure and shopping centre. Its emblem is the "maca", a tiny character with the mind of an inveterate rebel seen climbing the gates of the town hall. This is the birthplace of the great poet Maurice Carême who sang its praises in verse. There are a number of fine buildings, and a small history and archaeology museum illustrating the Roman occupation (see the villa opposite the Hosté Farm). The giants John and Alice, the Notre-Dame-de-Basse-Wavre Tower (on the Sunday after the Feast of St. John the Baptist) mark the local calendar of festive events. But Wavre also has one of the largest amusement parks anywhere in Europe, Walibi (from the names of the towns Wavre, Limal, and Bierges). Every year it opens its doors to one million visitors who follow in the footsteps of Tintin, visit Ali Baba's cave, and enjoy all the thrills of the "Tornado", the great wheel or the wild water run, to name but a few of the forty attractions.

Opposite and overleaf :
The Walibi Amusement Park.

La Ramée Farm in Jauchelette.

In **Limal**, a living museum houses some 450 species of aquatic plant. Its promoters have designed water gardens in places throughout the world.

Then you will be encouraged to stop for a while in places like **Mont-Saint-Guibert** (brewery), **Corbais, Corroy** (and their castle-farmsteads), **Chaumont-Gistoux** (two mills, and country sugar tarts and cheesecakes), **Bonlez** (castle, walks, Second World War Museum), **Biez** (panoramic views), **Grez-Doiceau** (Péruchet puppet museum, horseback procession on St. George's Day), **Tourinnes-La-Grosse** (fine church, presbytery, and cemetery on the hill, and Martinmas game in November), and **Beauvechain** (large air base). But stranger still are the sights mentioned below.

In **Glimes**, for example, a Gallo-Roman tumulus juts out of the countryside like a natural out-growth. It originally topped a grave. In **Jauchelette**, the Ramée Farm has the largest barn in the country. There is a former commandery of the Knights of Malta in **Huppaye**. Everywhere in the tiny blossoming Hesbaye Region, the farmhouses are majestic, some of them are fortified, and many of the farms are still worked today.

In **Folx-Les-Caves**, the caves are huge mushroom farms. From **Orp-Le-Grand**, you can take away a delicious type of green sausage made with curly cabbage. Not to be confused with a variation on the same theme made in Jodoigne ! Near **Pietrain**, which has given its name to a breed of black-spotted pig, is the provincial recreation centre of **Helecine** (castle, park, angling, walks, traditional folklore museum). **Jodoigne**, which is an agricultural and educational centre, is especially worth a visit for its narrow streets and fine buildings (St. Médard's Church, spiral steeple on Notre-Dame-du-Marché, and Ghobert, Pasture and La Vicomté castles). Some of them are made of the white limestone from Gobertange that characterises the most prestigious buildings in the Brabant.

"The other Brabant", which is typically Romanic, joins other rivers (Thyle, Thines, Samme, Senne and Sennette). There are "places worth a visit" in abundance.

Firstly, **Villers-La-Ville** is the starting point for the 62-mile aptly-named "Wanderer's Route" (Route Vagabonde).

The Cistercian abbey was one of the most prosperous in the Western world. Major restoration work is being undertaken on the ruins, to turn them into a spectacular cultural centre. As they stand, isolated in the depths of the forest, the ruins have lost nothing of their past grandeur; it is easy to imagine what they were once like. In the vicinity, you can see **Gentinnes** (missionary training centre), **Cortil-Noirmont** (French museum, pink farmhouse), **Walhain-Saint-Paul** (farms, ruins of the old fortress), **Grand-Leez** (mills), **Sart-Dames-Avelines** (bird sanctuary in the Thyle Marshes), and, as a reminder, Baisy Thy, said to be the birthplace of Godefroi de Bouillon.

Nivelles is the capital of the Romanic Country or 'Roman Païs'. In the 7th century, Gertrude founded the first convent in the country there. The collegiate church now bears her name. It has been entirely restored and is one of the finest expressions of Meuse-style Romanesque architecture. Austere, well-balanced and impressive (332 ft. long), it has a chancel, chapels, towers and turrets. Top of the list of treasures housed there are some sumptuous gold items (including the saint's reliquary). The archaeological basement contains the remains of Merovingian and Carolingian churches. Enjoy the

The ruins of the Abbey of Villers-la-Ville.

The nave of the collegiate church in Nivelles.

The superb Romanesque chevet of Nivelles' collegiate church.

tranquillity of the adjacent cloisters and look up to "John-John", the Jack-o'-the-clock that is the town mascot, said to have been given to the community by Charles the Bold. The archaeological museum, the Tourette Museum, the Recollect Chapel and the Simone Tower (once part of the town walls) complete the visit of a town that also has a green, flower-strewn, shady focal point - the Dodaine Park. The "Aclots" Town (the nickname of the population living within the walls, in contrast to the country-folk) is famous with gourmets for its "tarte al djote" (cheese, spinach-beet and herb pastry) and its "doubles" (cheese-filled buckwheat pancakes).

Now let's head for the two Braines. **Braine-L'Alleud** (Seven Fountains) and **Braine-Le-Château** in the Hain Valley. The last stocks left in the country, a reminder of feudal justice, stand on the main square near the church containing the alabaster tomb of Count Maximilien de Hornes. His family gave its name to the fine privately-owned castle hidden in the midst of a park. The Bailiff's House (16th-century) and the old communal mill (now a Milling Museum) form a harmonious group of buildings.

During September, there are major mediaeval events which attract large crowds.

Once you have passed Clabecq (it has a 19th-century steel complex that is quite exceptional in a rural area), you will reach **Tubize**. You can learn all about the town in the Musée de la Porte, a museum housed in an old Spanish

The Ronquières slope and its panoramic tower.

farm built on the remains of the mediaeval town walls. To the west lies **Saintes** (church, reliquary and procession in honour of St. Renelde), and to the south is **Quenast** (small-scale brewery) and its witless quarries of porphyry which have paved (with good intentions?) most of the main roads in Belgium and elsewhere.

Rebecq-Rognon, birthplace of Solvay (who developed an ammonia-soda process), has two main attractions - the Arenberg mills (a fine building laid out as a regional museum with temporary exhibitions) and the little Train of Happiness which wends its way through the Oiseaux (Birds') Valley in summer.

In **Ittré**, it is the forge-museum which attracts tourists while **Ronquières** is so well-known that it doesn't require an introduction. Its slope down to the Brussels-Charleroi canal is almost one mile

45

long and there is a 220-foot drop from top to bottom. The panoramic tower (open from May to the end of August) explains how it works and you can pay it a personal visit before you set off on a boat trip along the river. On your return, don't forget the peaceful village with its mill and 16th-century church. **Braine-Le-Comte**, quietly hemmed in by the Houssière Woods (footpaths and lakes) has a very attractive church (St. Géry's) and a few other 17th-century buildings.

After that, we are off to the two Ecaussines, firstly **Ecaussines-d'Enghien** and its Follie (or foliaged) Castle which is only open on request. The stained glass windows in the chapel are the work of Bernard Van Orley, painter to Emperor Charles V, who is buried in St. Rémy's Church. **Ecaussines-Lalaing**, the land of small granite quarries, stands in the shadow of its tall massive feudal castle, originally built in the 12th century. Its many rooms (including a remarkable kitchen) are really a series of small museums. In the village church is the grave of Blandina Rubens, the sister of the famous artist. On Whit Monday, a matrimonial snack brings together unmarried people of both sexes. It is the young ladies who take the initiative...The day ends in popular merrymaking. The Bridge of Sighs, the Lovers' Tunnel, and Sweet Arcades are the names of just some of the local beauty spots. The village is linked to Ronquières by the 3-mile Sennette Footpath.

Seneffe (Louis XVI castle on which restoration is now almost complete) takes us into the quite different Centre region in which La Louvière is the main industrial and business town. The ''she-wolf's town'' was the cradle of Belgian surrealism (Achille Chavée) but its energy is best

Hydraulic lifts.

The Château de la Follie in Ecaussines-d'Enghien.

expressed in its mid-Lent Sunday Carnival (there are some 500 behatted participants).

It is an excellent centre from which to tour the various places of interest in the region, in particular **Le Rouelx**, the birthplace of the preacher St. Feuillien (a beer has been named after him). Its main feature is the castle of the Princes of Croy, said to have as many windows as there are days in the year... Its salons are luxurious; its rose garden is unique (100,000 roses in the summer!) and its gardens contains 200 lime trees and a rare Lebanese Cedar. The **Canal du Centre**, which was built for economic reasons, runs through scenery that is often bucolic. If you've never seen canal barges take a lift, this is your chance ! Four hydraulic lifts (the oldest one dates from 1888) still work in Houdeng, Strépy and Thieu. They enable the barges to overcome the huge differences in level along the canal's length. They are carefully maintained by a worthy association which shows people round the lifts and the Canal House Museum.

The Mariemont Park.

Egyptian queen. Mariemont Museum

Mariemont gets its name from Mary of Hungary who had a castle built there. It was razed to the ground on several occasions. Remains of successive constructions can be seen as you stroll through a wonderful 35-hectare park that is also an open-air museum. The modern building houses the collections of the captain of industry and patron of the arts, Raoul Warocqué. All periods are represented from Antiquity onwards, with items from the Ming and Qing dynasties. The Royal Mariemont Museum, which is an exhibition and entertainment centre, fulfils its cultural role to the full.

After passing through the old village of **Saint-Vaast**, we get to **Binche**. Its name is synonymous with its carnival, one of the most beautiful and most authentically traditional anywhere in the world. It takes weeks to prepare and it lasts for three days up to and including Shrove Tuesday. And that is the only day you will see the "gilles", characters symbolising renewal who call upon the earth to be fertile and exorcise evil spirits. The "gille" wears a mask when he first appears and only dons his hat bedecked with ostrich feathers in the afternoon when his clogs ring out on the cobblestones of the main square while he hands out oranges galore to the crowds. The ritual is multisecular and fiercely protected. Just once in your life, you really must see the Binche Carnival! You will learn more about it from the former Augustine College that is now the unique Carnival and Mask Museum with exhibitions illustrating carnival traditions from all over the world. But Binche has more to offer than its "gilles". The town walls are the best preserved in Belgium given their exceptional length. The park encourages visitors to take a stroll in the shade of the impressive collegiate church of St. Ursmer's (interesting treasure) that protects the delightful St. Andrew's Chapel by its very massiveness. On the main square, the onion-towered belfry and the town hall form a harmonious group of Renaissance buildings.

Three miles away is the ancient abbey of **Bonne Espérance** (Good Hope), famous for its beer and bakery. And from there, we reach the largest of all Wallonia's towns - **Charleroi**. This industrial city on the banks of the R.Sambre, now a road and rail junction (with an airport at Gosselies), took the name of King Charles II of Spain in 1666. It is on ''his'' square that we see the town hall (belfry, wonderful museum of Walloon art) and St. Christopher's Basilica.

Charleroi's sights are first and foremost contemporary (Exhibition Centre, University of Work, Art Gallery). There is an upper and lower town, the latter reached by a large pedestrian precinct. The Glass Museum is worth a visit. Not only does it house very

The carnival in Binche.

An aerial view of Charleroi.

valuable collections from various historical periods, but it also has a clear presentation of this industrial art form throughout the world as well as in Belgium. The best way to visit Charleroi is on foot, and the town centre is not really very big. Why not spend a Sunday there and see the colourful busy market?

Charleroi has numerous ''satellite villages'', worth visiting mainly for their living folklore, mainly in the form of the Entre-Sambre-et-Meuse marches. The most characteristic of these is held in **Jumet**, on the nearest Sunday to 22nd July. The Madeleine Walk is processional. It celebrates the lady of the manor's recovery from the Black Death in 1380. This is a unique example of a dancing procession (symbolising joy). **Marcinelle**, which suffered one of this century's worst mining disasters in 1956, honours one of its sons in a one-room museum - the government minister and popular orator, Jules Destrées. This is also an international centre for the publication of cartoon strips. In **Fontaine-l'Eveque** there is a mining museum; in **Wanfercée Baulet**, a film museum; and in **Trazegnies** (17th-century castle), vines now grow on the disused rubbish dump.

In **Ligny**, on the road to Waterloo, Napoleon won his final victory two days before his downfall. And memories of the battle are everywhere, right down to the old ·bombard standing at the entrance to the village. Even better, there is a museum, a memorial, commemmorative plaques on the En Haut and En Bas farms. More importantly, there is a historic procession held on the first Sunday in July which helps to maintain the "Napoleonic cult". But it is a spectacle of a quite different type, something much more unusual, which strikes visitors most - the "Passion Game" (each Sunday in Lent) involving over a hundred actors and walk-on parts played by the villagers. On the edges of the Namur region and the Charleroi district, the vast Ligny Plain opens onto **Sombreffe** (Blücher's headquarters, and the Houssière Farm with its tower-dovecot), the tranquil villages of **Tongrinne**, **Bothey**, and **Mazy** (what fine farmsteads !). More impressive, austere and magnificent is the moated castle of **Corroy-le-Château**, which stands in the midst of a large park well hidden from prying eyes. It is flanked by seven machicolated towers and the furnishings are of the utmost elegance. This is a place that lends itself to cultural events. Then we come to **Gembloux** on the R.Orneau, once well-known for its cutlery industry. Its well-ordered former Benedictine abbey now houses a State Faculty of Agricultural Sciences that enjoys a very high reputation. In town there are countless reminders of the old community - the Bailiff's House, now the Cutlery Museum ; the Clock Tower ; St. Guibert's Church, and the statue

All these areas are used for agriculture and sturdy farms are dotted right across them. As you get nearer the Meuse, take a short stop at the castle in **Franc-Waret** which is well hidden from view in the midst of terraced gardens, meadows, woodland and lakes. It

The banks of the R.Sambre in Namur.

of the monk Sigebert etc. Be sure to try the local specialities - the abbey's beer and cheese, quiche, and giblotains.

Beyond Gembloux, the wide sweeps of the Hesbaye region spread lazily eastwards until they merge with their neighbours in the Brabant and the Liège Region where they catch up with the R.Mehaigne.

is a splendid residence, richly decorated and furnished.

We then pass through Gelbressée (Notre-Dame Church and sanctuary) to regain Namur. At the confluence of the rivers Sambre and Meuse, of which it is one of the most attractive daughters, **Namur** is the official capital of Wallonia and it occupies a central position within the region. Its

The fortress in Namur.

immediate surroundings of green countryside and rocks maintain the "town-in-the-heart-of-the-country" atmosphere that makes it so charming. A few treasures will encourage you to stay here just a bit longer, but visitors get as much enjoyment out of strolling through the old town, seeing the Saturday markets and the gigantic celebrations held during the first weekend in July ("Pantomime" and sales) and the third weekend in September (Wallonia Festival which takes over the entire town). When its shops indulge in extra events, they provide a stage for more authentic and living folklore - stilt-walkers (and their battles), the forty Molons from the Royal Moncrabeau Society (a musical and philanthropic association, King Liar competition !). In August, in **La Plante**, there are nautical jousting tournaments. In **Bouge**, halfway through Lent, you can see the largest "Great Bonfire" in Wallo-

nia. But let's come back to the town, dominated by its citadel, Europe's former "anthill", which has been subjected to innumerable sieges (twenty in as many centuries). Now used for more peaceful purposes, it is an attractive place to visit. You can see its sophisticated architecture and appreciate its past (Arms and Military History Museum). There is also a torchlight procession down into the subterranean passages, an audiovisual presentation, and a small train to take you round an 8-hectare site well away from civilisation, which you can reach by chairlift from the foot of the Champeau Hill. The road leading to it is described as "marvellous". It will take you to the Forest Museum (with arboretum) and will provide you with several high-class panoramic views. You will see the confluence of the two rivers and the slate roofs of the old houses along the quays, as well as the countless belltowers in the lower town. You can also admire the towers on St.Aubin's (or Alban's) cathedral, described by the poet Baudelaire as a "miniature St.Peter's", or on the Baroque St.Loup's Church, or on the Church of St.John the Baptist whose onion tower overlooks the picturesque Vegetable Market district where a meal in one of the many restaurants around the small square is always a pleasant experience.

As you stroll through the

The R.Meuse.

An aerial view of the fortress in Namur.

nearby pedestrian precincts, don't forget to look up at the fronts of the buildings (rue de l'Ange, rue de la Croix, rue des Fripiers). Namur is a centre of the arts and culture and it has its fair share of museums - Ancient Arts (fine items showing the goldsmith's craft), Félicien Rops (the "scandalous" painter, the seductive Fély who was born in Namur), the Diocesan Museum (treasure belonging to St.Aubin's Cathedral), the Groesbeck-de-Croix Residence (Decorative Arts), and the Archaeological Museum

Namur Casino.

(exhibits from the days of the Romans and the Franks). And, the finest of all the seven wonders of Belgium, the Treasure in Oignies Priory (late 12th century), kept by the Sisters of Notre-Dame in their convent.

Rue des Brasseurs, the Meat Market, the belfry, the parade ground (Place d'Armes), and the Marie Spilar Tower - just a few of the other places of interest at which you will no doubt stop when you visit this delightful provincial town that is so forward-looking and where "joie de vivre" is so obvious. It is, then, a playful town (there is a famous Casino on the banks of the Meuse), and one that enjoys its food ("avisances" and other pork-based products, oxtail soup etc.).

After leaving Namur, we can offer three suggestions - either head for its "hinterland", or for the borders of the Condroz Plateau, or travel along the banks of the Meuse to Dinant.

Firstly, then, the hinterland, on the banks of the Sambre with **Floreffe** and its important Premonstratensian abbey founded in 1121 by St.Norbert on a spur of rock.

The sanctuary and mill-brewery are open to the public (regional produce, and crafts). Further on is the small village of Tamines and the larger town of Auvelais-Sambreville. A few miles away is **Spy** and its caves where the skeletons of the Neanderthal-type "Man of Spy" were discovered (the walk is signposted). As you turn back towards Namur, you will see the farm belonging to Falnuée Castle (in Mazy) and the fortified castle of Mielmont (in Onoz) which provided shelter for Madame de Maintenon when Louis XIV laid siege to Namur.

In **Temploux**, the aerodrome

offers visitors numerous sports and tourist activities (plane and helicopter trips). It also provides top-class accommodation.

From Namur, the Meuse flows on to Andenne, passing through **Marche-les-Dames** and past the rocks where King Albert I died in a climbing accident on 17th February 1934. A small museum has been opened in sad memory of the monarch.

In Wallonia, nature is a constant source of surprise, even when you are least expecting it. In **Seilles**, a well-stocked nature reserve exists side-by-side with the industrial working of zinc and lead

The chancel in Floreffe Abbey.

Countryside in the Andenne region.

mines! This is the gateway to **Andenne** founded by St.Begge (12th-century collegiate church with a Canonesses' Museum). Two fountains, the small houses and tiny gardens once lived in by the canonesses, and others built of limestone dating from the 17th and 18th century all add their distinctive flavour to a town that forms a transition between the Namur and Liège regions. The Ceramics Museum serves as a reminder of an industry that has now died out but which was developed in the area as far back as Roman times. Andenne was also a famous and respected pipe-making centre. Its traditions, though, die hard - there is the Bear Carnival (Lent Sunday), named after Charles Martel (he was born here) who is said to have

slain a bear at the age of nine. The second weekend in July sees the International Folklore Festival and on Christmas night there is the "Trairies Game". People play cards for "cougnous", a sort of Christmas bun traditionally made by local pastrycooks.

The whole area is crisscrossed by a tourist route with a decidedly worrying name, the "Cow War Route" (la Guerre de la Vache). It serves as a reminder of the bloody disputes opposing the County of Namur and the Principality of Liège as the result of the theft of a cow in 1273.

From the banks of the Meuse to the heart of the Condroz. High-quality tourism, this, perhaps not to everybody's taste, but a pleasurable experience in a region which some people find

reminiscent of the Limousin in France.

Coutisse, Jallet, Perwez, Goesnes, Flostoy, Havelange with their mighty houses and large farmsteads are all on our route. But we'll pass through here at top speed. Into the Samson Valley where the river is capricious, quite a contrast to the unending lines of gently-rolling hills in the Con-

55

droz region. The first sight of rusticity awaits us in **Wierde** (small farms, defensive tower, Romanesque church). Then come the stone houses in **Mozet**, with its old manorhouse and castle. **Goyet** is a prehistoric site with a large number of dwellings. The caves are open to the public and contain representations of life in those far-off days. The fish-filled Samson (''Beaver Valley'') opens onto an amusement park in Thon-Samson which is sure to interest the younger members of the family. The castle in **Faulx-les-Tombes**, where Jean de La Fontaine is said to have stayed, always reminds visitors of Snow-White's Castle.

Gesves is one of the largest horse-riding centres in Belgium (all-inclusive courses, short courses, treks, riding).

Ciney considers itself to be the capital of the Condroz. It is a busy shopping centre, and its cattle market is worth a visit, any Friday at dawn. The town is made even livelier by the Antiques Fair, the Second-hand Furniture and Curios Fair and the Market. On its square is a delightful bandstand, and a collegiate church with a beautiful font. The macaroon tart and two types of beer (Cuvée de Ciney and Cinacienne) will leave you with their own memories of your visit.

Now we take the road through the Bocq Valley where the river tumbles and rushes along, and here we are in **Spontin** (thermal springs) where the feudal castle has a touch of Renaissance elegance. It is also a splendid museum. The masterpiece in **Crupet** is its 13th-century keep, a redoubtable and magnificent piece of architecture lapped by the river. But this famous Meuse village (with its endless walks) just as frequently attracts visitors for the St.Anthony caves decorated with multicoloured statues produced by the Valcouleurs workshops (pilgrimage on the Sunday after 13th June). Nearby, in landscapes that are more than reminiscent of the Ardennes, stands **Maillien** (Roman villas, Ronchinne Castle, rhododendron gardens).

◁ *The feudal castle in Spontin.*

Nowhere is the Meuse more beautiful and better-suited for tourism than in the Namur region where it is joined by numerous rivers and streams. Abbeys are almost as commonplace as castles. The old brick and stone villages, the rocks, the fortresses and good food all form a permanent flower garden on the banks of a river that continues peacefully

The keep in Crupet.

and romantically on its way. Dave (church, castle, old houses) has the largest island in the country, on the Meuse near the Néviaux Rocks that are sheer enough to delight any climber. In **Lustin**, it is the Frêne Rocks that, beyond the Tailfer Rock, plunge straight down into the Meuse (observation platform).

Godinne is another tourist cen-

tre in the valley (really everywhere is a tourist centre!).It stands on a meander of the Meuse. Its old centre dates from the 17th century (old farm, timbered houses, Spanish-style castle). In the summer, large numbers of exhibitions are held here. Leisure facilities measure up to modern requirements.

Yvoir is perhaps the most char-

ming of all the Meuse region summer holiday resorts, set as it is amongst woods and rocks, with its island (water sports) accessible by a ferry and the natural oasis (nature reserve and Champalle Castle - slide shows, training centre, botanic gardens, environmental courses, ornithological revalidation centre). The ruins of Poilvache Castle, one of the largest

57

Water-skiing near Wépion on the R.Meuse.

fortresses in the County of Namur, overlook the Meuse from a distance. As you arrive in Dinant, you will see **Leffe** Abbey which still has a few buildings dating from the 17th and 18th centuries; the others have been rebuilt. The Fonds de Leffe Route is a pleasant little road. Beauty

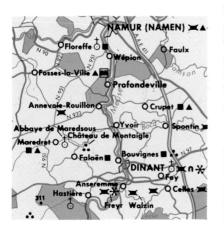

spots are even more numerous along the left bank (the more "comfortable" road).

After Namur comes **Wepion**, capital of the "imperial" strawberry growing area - imperial for its rotundity, size, and taste (Museum of Strawberries and Local Agriculture, events held during the first weekend in July). Opposite the Néviaux Rocks and Dave's island, a remarkable towpath 3 miles long provides visitors with a riverside walk. On the hill are the remains of the Marlagne Estate with the small chapel in which the Brotherhood of the Fox and the Strawberry meets on the first Saturday in September.

Fosses-la-Vieille, at equal distance from the Sambre and the Meuse, was founded by an Irish monk named Feuillen. The collegiate church (it has its own treasure) bears his name, as does the

traditional procession held once every seven years (1991) which is unusual among the Entre-Sambre-et-Meuse Marches because it is not an annual event (2,500 participants, with a hundred on horseback). But the carnival takes place every year, at Mid-Lent. It has its own star characters - the "doudou" (hunchback) and the "Chinels" (an abbreviation of "polichinelle", or Mr. Punch). It also has its traditional music. Also worth a visit in Fosses, is the Small Chapter Museum (costume dolls).

And back we go to the Meuse via **Profondeville**, a major water-skiing centre (beginners' courses, events and competitions). **Rivière** on the hill provides a surprising panoramic view over the "seven Meuses", so-called because of the number of meanders at this point !

Annevoie is not to be missed. It has an elegant and beautifully austere castle, once the property of the Counts of Montpellier. It is also popular for its gardens, one of the main tourist attractions in Wallonia. They are a balanced blend of formal, English cottage and Italian styles and there are numerous natural waterfalls and fountains. Yes, natural - there is no machinery to make them work !

Statues, arbours, grottoes, sculptures, and temporary exhibitions bring life and movement to

Annevoie - château and fountains.

Opposite, top to bottom :
The charming village of Falaen,
the ruins of Montaigle,
and Maredsous Abbey.

◀ *Two views of the gardens*
in Annevoie.

12 hectares of garden that are floodlit on summer evenings.

In Anhée, the R. Molignée flows into the Meuse. But we shall leave the river for a while to see a few sights such as the ruins of **Montaigle** (13th century) that are constantly being restored. Many legends are associated with the castle, including the one about Midone de Bioul who died from a swordthrust delivered by her own father when she tried to run between him and her fiancé during a duel.

In **Falaën** there is a castle-farm with great square towers. The right wing has been turned into an exhibition centre. The pretty little village of Sosoye (blue stone houses) takes us to **Maredsous**, the famous 19th-century Benedictine abbey built in a style that is both pure and austere. Visitors can try bread, beer and cheese, all of them bearing the abbey's name. It is also a hostel and study cen-

tre. The Grégoire-Fournier Centre is used for exhibitions. The abbey church is also open to the public and you can attend sung Mass. Then try a walk to **Maredret** where the castle is now used as a Benedictine monastery. This is also the woodcraft village (museum, craft shops, and workshops). Other Benedictines have settled in **Ermeton-sur-Biert**. Then go on to **Furnaux** so that you can admire the black marble font, a masterpiece of 12th-century Meuse-region art!

The entire Molignée Valley can be visited in a pleasant char à banc that travels at its own tranquil speed. If you have some time at your disposal, extend your visit to take in Florennes (ramparts, castle, collegiate church) and Mettet (17th-century limestone houses, St.Roch's Chapel, Foy farm and the car racing circuit).

We come back to the Meuse in **Bouvignes** with its 16th-century Spanish house (now a fine museum), its richly-decorated St.Lambert's Church, and its picturesque old town rebuilt after being ransacked in 1554 by French troops led by Henri II.

It was these same troops who also demolished **Crèvecœeur Castle**. From the top there is now a splendid view of the Meuse Valley.

Along with Huy, **Dinant** is the prettiest of all the Meuse's daughters, according to Victor Hugo. One thing's for sure - it's the queen of tourism in the Meuse region! And justifiably so. The town famous for its spun copper and its good food (for example the "flamiche" or full fat cheese and butter tart served piping hot, or its pastry and honey "couque"), the town where the locals are called "copères" (coppersmiths), is always bustling and

Dinant - the fortress
and the collegiate church.

△
The banks of the R.Meuse
in Dinant.

A view from the fortress.▷

bubbling with comings-and-goings. There are natural features worth a visit ("The Marvel" cave discovered in 1904 and the "Mont-Fat" cave with the chamber dedicated to the worship of the goddess Diana, the Bayard Rock or Step that is 114 ft. high and whose wall, through which Louis XIV's troops hacked their way, is said to have been split open by the hoof of one of the Four Aymon Boys' horses!). There are architectural sights too (the Citadel 325 ft. above the river, which was besieged 17 times; the Arms and Weapons Museum accessible from the road

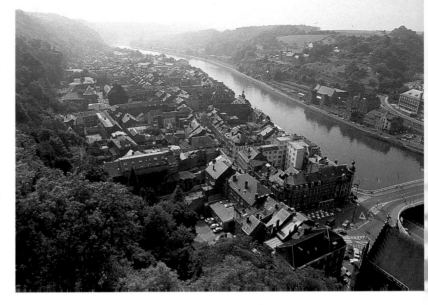

The Bayard Rock commands the entrance to Dinant.

The R.Lesse, overlooked by the Château de Walzin.

or by cable car or by 408 steps leading up from behind the Notre-Dame collegiate church with the strange bulbous belltower containing some fine pieces of local copper work and other masterpieces). There are also countless shops, a casino that has been renovated throughout, cruises on the Meuse (to Namur or Givet) and an excellent infrastructure for sports activities and accommodation, just to complete the picture!

The Dinant Region is a must for visitors. Take the strange church in **Foy-Notre-Dame** for example. Its coffered ceiling includes 147 paintings representing scenes and saints from the Gospels (there is a procession from Rochefort to Foy on Whit Monday). Or **Furfooz** and its national park high up on a rocky plateau riddled with caves and caverns that are of major archaeological interest. The R.Lesse offers sports enthusiasts an opportunity to canoe from **Houyet** to **Anseremme**. A number of hire companies cater for one-day sportsmen (car park in

The R.Lesse has carved out some superb places for canoeing.

The rock wall in Freyr.

Anseremme, with train link to Houyet). The most famous sights are the "Aiguilles de Chaleux" and Walzin Castle high up on a sheer wall of rock. If you still have some energy left when you arrive at your destination, use it for one of the walks that take you to the Moniat Rocks or the Colébi Ravine, the village of Falmignoul, Celles church, or **Veves** Castle with its five "pointed" towers. It is said to be more than twelve centuries old (museum). On the other side of the valley in the middle of a park is **Noisy Castle** (19th-century English style, now a museum and a nature study centre for school parties).

Freyr is well-known as the best rock-climbing centre in Wallonia. From the top of its scarp slopes,

you can see the 18th-century Meuse-region castle with its waterfalls and orange grove. It is said that Louis XIV discovered a new drink here in 1675 - coffee. The Meuse, which is particularly wild at this point, wends and bends its way to **Waulsort** on its ·left bank. This is an outstanding beauty spot. The marina caters for the many small craft that sail the river. All that remains of the abbey built in the 10th century is a palace-castle. The rocks ("The Flag" and "The Dog") are also suitable for climbing; they lie in the shadow of the ruined Castle Thierry.

The two Hastières make a fine pair ! **Hastière-Par-Dela** has a beautiful, massive Romanesque church, beneath the Tahaux

rocks. **Hastière-Lavaux** is linked to it by a bridge. This is a small but bustling and very popular holiday resort. It is especially busy because of the many holiday villages hidden among the hills beside the river. In the Féron Valley, the Pont-d'Arcole caves are as interesting for the experienced pot-holer as they are for the inexperienced tourist.

Towards the French frontier, there are still more places to visit - Blaimont (views over the Meuse and the Condroz Plateau), Soulme (grey stone houses), Gochenée, Agimont and the "18 villages" view, Heer and Minouche, its local hero represented by a kindly giant. But here we are almost out of Belgium altogether !

LIEGE, GATEWAY TO THE ARDENNES

Liège is the most flawless town in Wallonia. Liège and its vicinity are like fire and water. A mysterious alliance of opposites. Liège is liberty down the ages, regardless of the cost in lives lost, jealously guarding its independence as an episcopal principality. Liège is Charlemagne. Liège is Simenon. Liège, the town of scientists and artists. The frenzied nights of the "Carré" and the rich tranquillity of its one hundred churches. The historical heartland and the rough-and-tumble of its working class districts. The beautiful solitary parks and the crowded sports stadiums. Soul and spirit. Crystal and pewter. A crossroads in the heart of Europe, the gateway to the Ardennes, the "Hot-blooded City". Not something you can get to know in a single day. You really have to give it a bit more time ! Look round the hills of the Citadel, discover the majestic R.Meuse which flows through it, bringing its own particular rhythm as it wends its way between the seven hills. You reach the citadel by the astonishing Montagne de Bueren staircase (407 steps) or by the delightful rue Pierreuse and rue du Péry. Once back down "on ground level", take a walk round the "historical heart of the city" - the Ilôt Saint Georges (Museum of Walloon Art and exhibition hall), old houses in Féronstrée, the Ansembourg Museum (local 18th-century furniture), the Arms and Weapons Museum (the second-largest in the world), the Curtius Museum (archaeology and decorative arts, with Bishop Notger's prayerbook, a masterpiece of Romanesque art). There is also

The heart of Liège at nightfall.

The Arms Museum.

The font in Saint-Barthélemy. ▷

A typical interior,
Museum of Walloon Life. ▷

the admirable Glass Museum (10,000 items on show from one of the richest collections anywhere in the world).

Take one of the countless alleyways and cul-de-sacs in this attractive district and you will reach St. Bartholomew's Church whose Romanesque baptismal font by Renier du Huy is one of the "seven wonders of Belgium". A haven of silence just two steps away from the noisy Hors-Château (splendid façades) can be enjoyed in the Architecture Museum and the study of the most famous violinist of his day, Eugène Isaye who was born in Liège. A few yards away is the "Maram" (the Museum of Religious and Meuse-region art) and the Museum of Walloon Life in the former Minorite monastery. Each room is devoted to one aspect of life in days gone by as well as to Wallonia's folklore. It is a living, attractive "conservatory". There is an admirable reconstruction of a mining gallery, and a puppet theatre stages regular performances (there are still two other theatres of this type in Liège with the two most typically liégois of all characters, Tchantchès and his wife Nanesse, as well as Charlemagne, Roland, the gallant Knights and the evil Saracens). The round trip ends with the Place Saint-Lambert and Place du Marché. On the first of these squares, which is constantly the scene of road works etc., stands the superb Palace of Prince-Bishops which now houses

The Prince-Bishops' Palace.
Above : *the main façade.*
Opposite : *the great
inner courtyard.*

the law courts and Provincial Government offices. The first courtyard has 60 bulbous columns, all of them different; the second, smaller one is a sort of rustic cloister. On the Place du Marché (flower, fruit and vegetable market), the "Perron" (a fountain topped by a column) symbolises local liberty. It stands opposite the town hall, a fine 18th-century building nicknamed "the violet".

Along the banks of the Meuse is "la Batte" (or "quay" in Liège dialect). Every Sunday morning, a popular market attracts large crowds. A sight not to be missed ! The former Meat Market and the 16th-century Havart House ("Old Liège") are worth a look.

The town's shopping centre occupies a huge pedestrian precinct area. The Opera House ("Theatre Royal"), the wide boulevards, and some remarkable churches (St.Paul's Cathedral, collegiate church of St.John, churches of St.James, St.Denis and the Holy Cross, and St.Martin's Basilica) can all be seen as you stroll along. The Avroy Park to the south leads to the "Terrasses" which are decorated with 14

Opposite and below :
The Batte Market on the banks of the R.Meuse.

A panoramic view of Liège.

bronze sculptures including "Li Torai" ("the bull", the university students' emblem). One of the bridges over the Meuse takes you

The "Perron"
on the Place du Marché.

to the Conference Centre (built 1958) in the Boverie Park, once the botanical gardens (rose garden, and a Museum of Modern Art with the largest collection of French works in the country). We are now on the right bank, "Across the Meuse", between the river itself and its backwater. This is the protesters' district par excellence. It celebrates a "Free Republic" and a "Free Commune" every 15th August — procession, entertainments, local aquavit tasting (the local brew is known as "pèkêt"), and much eating of "boukètes", (thick buckwheat pancakes). The house of the composer André-Modeste Grétry (the greatest of all Liège's musicians alongside César Franck) is open to the public and there is a signposted route taking you in the footsteps of Georges Simenon who lived in this district for twenty years.

Liège is protected by its hills and their open spaces, in particular in Cointe and Le Sart-Tilman

where Liège University has gradually been developing since the late 1970's (botanic gardens, open-air museum, walks, Colonster Castle and its Simenon Foundation, a personal gift from the writer).

To the north of the town, the Albert Canal flows into the Meuse and unites it with the Schelde, just as Liège is linked to Antwerp. The R.Meuse flows on to the Netherlands, through **Jupille** (largest brewery in Belgium), **Herstal** (famous armaments factory and local museum in what was once the residence of Pippin the Short and Charlemagne), and **Visé**, the last town in the Belgian Meuse. The collegiate church of St. Martin contains St.Hadelin's reliquary (procession on third Sunday in September).

St.Paul's Cathedral, in the heart
of the pedestrian precinct. ▷

River traffic on the Meuse.

But Visé is especially worth a visit for its traditional events based on the guilds which maintain a well-developed sense of joint competition. The Crossbowmen (founded 1310), the Arquebusiers (founded 1579) and the Free-Arquebusiers (1909) honour their patron saints George and Martin with great dignity and organise shooting competitions. Moreover, each guild has its own museum. The local culinary speciality is "goose after the fashion" (oie à l'instar) which one of the brotherhoods is trying to bring back into the limelight. The surrounding villages are very attractive (in Argenteau there is a privately-owned castle and fish-filled lakes fed by the R.Julienne). In Lanaye, there is the **Montagne Saint Pierre**, a nature reserve on a hill overlooking the Meuse sporting flowers more often seen in southern climes. The six villages in the Fouron, which are part of the Flemish Limburg, are mainly and sentimentally Walloon. Their landscapes are a blend of meadows, plains and small hills.

They complete the Herve Region, which is famous for its powerfully odorous cheese and its syrup.

The gently-rolling Herve Region, a paradise of green woods, copses and orchards (fruit trees, hawthorn hedgerows) is a "Little Normandy". The farmsteads are set wide apart, like the villages that are often still untouched by progress. **Herve** is the centre of the region (cavalcade, a long traditional procession held on Easter Monday). **Aubel** (the ancient heart of the region, numerous walks). **Mortroux** (wheel and cheese museum, Berwinne

narrow-gauge railway). The railway takes you to the **Val Dieu Abbey** founded in 1216 and rebuilt on several occasions. It is used for concerts, is open for visits and sells local produce. **Bolland** (castle-farm and presbytery). **Dalhem** (formerly a walled town, capital of a county, has an old keep, the ruins of the castle, and the town walls). **Clermont-sur-Berwinne** (remarkable 17th and 18th-century architecture). All these villages, and more besides, are among the most picturesque in the country. **Blegny** has turned its old colliery (closed in 1980) into a tourist complex. Former miners guide visitors round an underground gallery, the slag heap, and the machinery above ground. A huge leisure centre is developing around the major attraction and the visit is combined with a cruise on the R.Meuse (from Liège to Visé) and a trip on the local tramway ("Li Trimbleu") that wends its way through the fields. From there, you can go on to **Wegimont** and its provincial estate (castle catering for party bookings, seven lakes, arboretum, and swimming pool) and then to the Vesdre Valley.

Top : *Woodland and pastures in the Herve region.*

Middle : *A visit to the former coalfields in Blégny.*

Bottom :
the "Li Trimbleu" in Blégny.

CHEESE

"Apart from French cheese, there are three great cheeses in the world - Swiss Vacherin, English Stilton and Belgian Herve." (*"La Reynière"*)

The Belgian cheese, which has existed since the days of "The Romance of the Rose", comes from Wallonia and is named after the area of pasture and woodland that produces it. But there are dozens of others, of varying

degrees of hardness and with a variety of different rinds (hard, semi-hard, soft).

Particular mention must be made of the independent and highly-diversified production of goat's milk cheese. Fortunately, the consumption of this type of cheese within the families that produce them is increasing regularly. And restaurant owners include them in their menus. Some have even made a speciality of combinations of beer and cheese.

COMITE DE PROPA-GANDE DES FROMAGES DE WALLONIE
(Wallonia Cheese Information Board)
rue de Verviers 26
4651 Battico.
Tel. 087/67.44.97
087/67.50.77

Chaudfontaine Casino.

Chaudfontaine is the most important place ; it has been used for taking the waters since the 17th century. The water gushes out at body temperature. The Spring Park (Sauveur House and fountains) is elegantly laid out opposite the modern casino. On the hilltop, the Chèvremont Basilica and its chapel have been places of pilgrimage since 1688. Once there, you can enjoy a well-known local dish (an omelette containing Ardennes bacon and sausage), the just reward for all your efforts in climbing the Thier Notre-Dame and its Stations of the Cross. We follow the Vesdre to **Verviers**, once an international textile centre. The town has suffered from the decline of the woollen industry but its appearance and the mentality of the people still bear the marks of this former prosperity. Timbered houses, craftsmen's dwellings or bourgeois residences from centuries past stand on the banks of the R.Vesdre. The Grand Theatre, the Place des Martyrs, the Harmonie reception room, Notre-Dame Church, St.Lambert's Chapel, the Art Gallery and Museum of Ceramics, the town hall and Place du Marché, the very interesting Wool Museum and the Museum of Archaeology and Folklore will all encourage you to spend just a little more time here. Near Christmas, the Archaeology and Folklore Museum holds a "Verviers Bethlehem" during which tiny wooden statues are used to play out (in the Walloon language) 21 scenes from the childhood of Jesus. And as regards food, Verviers Cake and, even better, the rice tart will be sure to delight those with a sweet tooth. Verviers is also a good starting point for trips to the

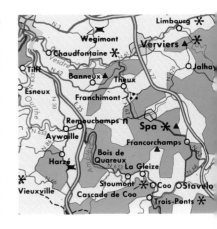

Verviers Town Hall.

deserves its nickname of "wonder of wonders".

L'Amblève (perhaps meaning the "water of alders"?) is the river with the greatest number of legends and mysteries to its credit. Its winding course has created unusually fine beauty spots. In the **Fond de Quareux,** for example, where huge quartzite blocks carpet the river bed. Likewise in the Chadière Valley, or Ninglinspo, or the "Congo". The numerous tributaries are all just as charming, especially the R.Liennes, with Lierneux, Chevron, Lorcé and the source of the R.Bru (mineral water). Or again there is **Stoumont** (panorama known as the "Congo"), **La Gleize** (old Ardennes houses, the royal Tiger, a Second World War tank in memory of a period during which the entire region

Fagnes region and the Gileppe Dam.

In the immediate vicinity lies **Limburg,** tne former ducal capital, with a gently-sloping cobbled square surrounded by old houses. The town still has its walls from which there is an exceptional view of the Vesdre Valley crossed by the impressive Dolhain Viaduct, as well as the Hertogenwal, and the Herve Region.

In Pépinster, the Vesdre is swollen by the waters of the R.Hoëgne which flows down from Theux (fountain, beautiful old market square) at the foot of the ruined castle of **Franchimont**. It was from here that 600 brave men set out in 1468 and were massacred in Liège by the army of Charles the Bold. The ruins have been skilfully preserved and restored. During odd-numbered years, a mediaeval "Frankish Fair" is held here. **Polleur** (timbered houses, Cuckoo Festival on the last Sunday in July) also lies on the banks of the R.Hoëgne.

From Theux, we follow part of the hilly route taken by the oldest of all cycle races, the Liège-Bastogne-Liège (Mont-Theux and Forges Hills). **Banneux** is not far away. It was there that the Virgin Mary appeared eight times to a poor child in 1933. Hundreds of thousands of pilgrims now visit the town every year. An international gathering of gypsies has also chosen this spot for its meeting. In **La Reid** (its woods were used by the Resistance forces), there is a game forest. In **Deigne,** there is the "Wild World" Safari Park and a village decked with flowers. It is the scene of much merrymaking at the end of July. After following the Chantoirs Valley (swallowholes, abysses, depressions hollowed out by water, we reach the Amblève Valley in Aywaille. The **Remouchamps** caves enable visitors to enjoy the longest underground boat trip anywhere in the world, on the Rubicon - almost half-a-mile in a small craft! It fully

Concretions in the Remouchamp Cave.

The Coo chairlift and, opposite, the waterfalls.

suffered major fire damage and much loss of life, and the December 44 Museum which is also a memorial to this period). Then there is **Coo** and its famous waterfalls above which runs a chair lift. There is an extensive open-air amusement park, **Tele-coo**, along the edge of the beauty spot.

Trois-Ponts gets its name from the three rivers that flow through it (R.Amblève, R.Salm and R.Baleur). It is a well-equipped holiday resort and the hills around it can best be visited by following the "panoramic view route" (Circuit des Panoramas) that runs through the attractive

The last remains of Stavelot Abbey.

Opposite : *The Blancs-Moussis, mid-Lent Carnival.*

village of Arbrefontaine (wayside cross, Ardennes houses). **Trois-Ponts**, a ski resort, is also the place for donkey rides. Finally, here we are in **Stavelot**, the seat of the former abbey principality of Stavelot/Malmédy. The old abbey founded by St.Remacle is the scene of a summer drama festival (July) and a music festival (August). It also has the Guillaume Apollinaire Museum, for the poet stayed here and fell in love in the town in 1899. A Museum of Religious Art and Local History (with a section devoted to tanning which made the town prosperous for four hundred years). There is also the Museum of the Spa-Francorchamps Circuit housing more than forty prestigious vehicles from every age in an ever-changing exhibition. Stavelot, which is the town of St.Remacle (see his reliquary in the parish church) is also the town of the "Blancs Moussis", characters in disguise (hilarious long-nosed masks, white canvas costumes, white bonnets, and immaculate white cape), the merry heroes of the very well-known mid-Lent carnival.

79

Opposite : *The Spa-Francorchamps racing circuit.*

Stavelot, then, encompasses much of the **Spa-Francorchamps Circuit**, which is partly open to the public. This is the finest national circuit in the world and the scene of Formula 1 racing, 24-hour car and motor bike races, the motor bike Grand Prix and other important competitions. It lies on the upper plateaux of the Ardennes at the gateway to the Fagnes. The nearby villages of

Spa Casino.

ster, Sart-lez-Spa (magnificent square with fountain) and Salwaser are typical of the Ardennes region.

Spa is well-known for its waters and its thermal cures. It was very popular with the world's upper crust as early as the 17th century and is justifiably nicknamed 'Europe's Café''. Its name has been taken into English to signify a place in which to take the waters. All the woodlands round about (there are 1240 miles of waymarked footpaths) are full of springs and fountains of sparkling water. These days, it is a very lively little town with a casino, a good tourist infrastructure, interesting crafts (the ''jolites'' or decorated objects using local Spa wood), interesting museums (the Spa Museum and the Horse Museum), some fine buildings (like the baths, the small games pavilion in the town's 7 Heures Park).

A local train will take you round the neighbouring hills where the scenery is totally unspoilt. To the Tahanfagne arboretum perhaps, or the Bérinzenne Forest, or the Warfaz Lake. The Artists' Walk is the most romantic and pleasant outing anyone could wish for.

Falcons' Rock and its panoramic view over the R.Ourthe.

It is in Liège that the R.Ourthe finishes its long course and flows into the Meuse. The Lower Ourthe (down to La Roche) is perfect for tourism. It is the river that made **Tilff** the old lady of tourism in the Liège area with the "Porês" Carnival on mid-Lent Sunday, the unique Bee Museum in the outbuildings of the castle, rocks suitable for climbing, and the Prés de Tilff leisure park. With **Esneux**, it has countless castles and some delightful hamlets. In Esneux, the Mary Park (arboretum) is one of the many places to head for on an outing. After Poulseur come the three

Comblain, "au-Pont" (large number of natural geological sites classified as the "Tartines", cave), "La-Tour" once famous for its International Jazz Festival, and "Fairon" (fine houses built of local stone). After leaving Comblain-au-Pont, at the confluence of the rivers Ourthe and Amblève, you may like to follow the Amblève up to **Aywaille**, an excursion centre and the home of the Four Aymon Boys (ruins of Amblève Castle). Sights include Dieupart Church, and **Harzé Castle** (1647) with a Meuse-region Renaissance façade and a Count's Chamber lined with Cordova lea-

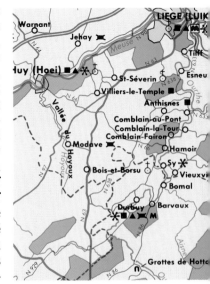

82

ther, not forgetting the Flour-Milling Museum.

We rejoin the R.Ourthe in **Hamoir**, a very popular summer holiday resort. Nearby on the R.Néblon is **Xhignesse** with its Romanesque church and old lime trees, then **Ferrières** whose old abbey lies hidden in the midst of the forest. The countryside in the **Sy Region** (sheer limestone rocks) has inspired generations of artists. **Vieuxville** is an estate in itself. La Bouverie Farm (1570) is now a riding stable and exhibition centre. Take a look, too, at the ruins of the fortress, the lair of the "Wild Boar of the Ardennes", Guillaume de la Marck. The castle stands over 280 ft. above the river. The Palogne farm and "gîte" provide sports amenities and leisure activities. Once you reach Bomal, you are in the Luxemburg province, in the Ourthe-et-Aisne region where the villages are twinned with villages in Beaujolais. This is one of the most popular holiday areas in Ardennes. Every year round 1st May, **Bomal** organises Beaujolais Festivals and every Sunday in the summer there is a "Petite Batte" an impressive market specialising in second-hand furniture and curios. In Villers-Sainte-Gertrude, the castle has been turned into accommodation and a tourist centre. As to the R.Aisne, one of the most capricious waterways in Ardennes, its valley will take you down to Juzaine, Heyd, and Mormont. in **Erezée**, you can climb aboard the T.T.A. (the Aisne Tourist Tram) which will show you the more rugged side of the valley in all its splendour. **Tohogne** has some exceptional murals in its Romanesque church. **Bar-**

Top : *Canoeing on the R.Ourthe.*

Bottom : *Rock climbing in Sy.*

Durbuy.

vaux, at the junction of the Condroz, Famenne and Ardennes regions, swarms with visitors in summer - the advantages of the town as well as the delights of the country, you might say. Not far away, in **Oppagne** and **Wéris**, impressive dolmens bear witness to the Stone Age. A "Gallic" festival is held there in August. Don't forget to visit the tiny Romanesque church before heading for **Durbuy**, the smallest town in the world. It's a real gem, a Lilliput with everything you could possibly need - castle, church with a music festival, corn market, Spanish House, good food, beauty spots, a small local train, the International Strip Cartoon Festival (in October), floral

"eat up" (at 3 m.p.h.) the local road network. Why not go to **Deulin**, for example, to see the beautiful, austere country castle that is now a centre for woodcraft and cabinet-making. It stands in a park-arboretum with many rare trees.

Hotton has the last cave to be discovered in Belgium (1958), the cave of the Thousand and One Nights, and by no means the least interesting. The town's architecture (including an old mill still in working order) and the natural features resulting from the local karst add their own charm to this small but busy town that is very much a tourist centre.

The Lower Ourthe flows down to Rendeux and **Marcourt** (goat's cheese, hermitage, birthplace of

Huy old town.

floats and carpets (in August), and events to celebrate the Feast of St.Hubert. In short, a busy place all year round. In the Ferme de la Tour in **Grand-Han**, you can hire a gipsy caravan hitched up to a solid Belgian horse and

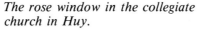
The rose window in the collegiate church in Huy.

Théroigne de Méricourt, who was one of the principal spiritual leaders of the French Revolution).

Huy is a place of many faces. As the "daughter of the Meuse", it provides a transition between Condroz and Hesbaye, three regions that complement each other well. As one of the oldest towns in the Principality of Liège, Huy traditionally had four wonders - the Pontia (the bridge over the Meuse which now no longer exists), the Rondia (the rose window in the collegiate church), the Tchiestia (fortress which was demolished to make way for the fort we see today) and the Bossinia (the fountain on the main square topped by the popular

Huy is noted for its pewter.

local character, the "cwèrneu" or "Good fellow"). The town is also a major centre for pewter plate on both banks of the R.Meuse (Batta House, the former Oultremont Hospice, St.Mengold's Church, the old cloth-hall, and the Minorite monastery). The old monastery has been turned into a local museum. This is where you discover that Huy was a major wine-growing community (the wine was called "Briolet") until the outbreak of the First World War. In addition to the Rondia, the collegiate church houses a remarkable treasure. Just beside it, the "Bethlehem" or former entrance to the canons' cloisters has some unique bas-reliefs. A chairlift takes visitors up to the Sarte Plateau where there is a leisure park

and Notre-Dame Chapel (pilgrimages).

In the Meuse Valley round Huy, there is no shortage of places to visit. **Amay** (Romanesque collegiate church), **Jehay-Bodegnée** (checkerboard castle with open-air museum, archaeological and pot-holing collections, very fine furniture), **Stockay** (Warfusée Castle), Aigremont (18th-century castle built on a spur of rock overlooking the Meuse), **Ramioul** (prehistoric caves and museum of prehistory), **Val-Saint-Lambert** (famous crystal works founded in 1826 in the former abbey; the chapter house has been restored).

As for **La Hesbaye**, it sits astride three provinces - Liège, Namur and Walloon Brabant. And wherever you look, there is a vast agricultural plain with impressive farmsteads. A tourist area where the sights may not be spellbinding and the architectural heritage is not outstanding but where you have to take time to enjoy the simple things in life. The two walled towns in the liégois Hesbaye are **Waremme** and **Hannut**. The two main rivers are the Mehaigne and the Burdinale. There are countless typical villages, two of the most attractive being Warnant-Dreye and Huccorgne. In **Oteppe**, the "L'Hirondelle" holiday centre and its castle stand deep in the forest. **Fallais** is a skilful example of a fortress built in a plain. As for the remainder, each place has its own hidden wonders and the natural environment has been particularly well researched and preserved in the Burdinale Nature Reserve.

It is the **Condroz** that encircles Huy. This is one of the plateaux in the Lower Ardennes, a fertile

Opposite, top :
The Château de Vervoz.

Opposite, bottom :
The Château de Jehay.

area of limestone and schist. Villages are remarkable for the opulence of the houses, farms, manors and churches. Needless to say, we cannot list them all. **Anthisnes** and its ''Avouerie'', a farm that is fortified like the other buildings in the hamlet. **Ocquier** and the enchantingly romantic **Vervoz** (lake, castle, chapel), **Modave** and the castle that once belonged to the Counts of Marchin, now in the heart of a bird sanctuary. It overlooks the R.Hoyoux whose waters were brought here by a system using a hydraulic wheel built by the Walloon carpenter Rennequin Sualem, who installed another identical wheel in Versailles (the Marly machine). The Hoyoux that flows through here is the coldest and clearest river in the country. And you must stop in Vyle, Tharoul, Seny, Bois-et-Borsu (frescoes in the Romanesque church), Vierset-Barse, and Les Avins (permanent outdoor sculpture exhibition). Not forgetting Villers-le-Temple, where there is a commandery of the Order of the Knights Templar. And be sure not to miss **Saint-Séverin**, a typical village with a Romanesque church that was once part of the Cluny priory - it is a pure architectural marvel.

◁The Château de Modave.

The magnificent chevet of Saint-Séverin Church.▷

BEER

The great poet Emile Verhaeren once wrote that ''The brewer is king in his village; the mayor is merely a prince'' - which just shows the importance placed on a profession that used to be very widespread.

In the years since the war, the economic climate has caused breweries to regroup. In Wallonia, there are now only a few left, the largest being the one in Jupillé/Liège that is a major name on the international market. These days, Belgians still down an average of more than 275 pints of beer per year (per inhabitant). Three-quarters of the production is a light, frothy, golden coloured beer called ''pils'' which is widely exported throughout Europe. The remaining one-quarter of the production concerns the so-called ''special'' beers, sold under more than 100 labels! The ''noblest'' of them all are the Trappist beers made by the monks themselves and subject to a (strictly) controlled high-quality label of origin. There are only six in the world, five of them in Belgium and three of those in Wallonia - Chimay, Orval and Rochefort. Not to be confused with beers that are monastery-made or monastery-orientated. More commonplace, and very tasty even if they are not ''traditional'', are the many beer-based recipes (especially kidney and rabbit, but they also include fish and, strange as it may seem, desserts such as sabayon). Beer cellars, equiped with the appropriate glasses, are beginning to spring up here and there. Certain strong beers are wonderful to drink with the cheeses that so many wines are not full-bodied enough to accompany.

CONFEDERATION DES BRASSERIES DE BELGIQUE (Belgian Brewers' Confederation) Grand-place 10 - 1000 Brussels. Tel. 02/511.98.68 02/511.49.87

THE « FAR EAST »

An arid region with a rugged climate and huge "desolate" wastes reminiscent, in some respects, of the Nordic plains of Scandinavia - this is the Hautes Fagnes Plateau in the east of the province of Liège. "Our very own Siberia", wrote the singer, Julos Beaucarne. In winter, others see it rather as a sort of "Belgian Canada". This is the roof of Belgium, the highest peak (a rather daring description!) being the

Signal de Botrange which culminates at 2,255 ft. This is nature at its most severe. It still bears traces of the Arctic flora and fauna that emigrated southwards to our regions during the great ice ages several thousand years ago. La Fagne is first and foremost the

Scenery in the Hautes-Fagnes.

peat bogs created by the slow rotting down of sphagnum, a sort of saturated moss that can grow several feet deep. La Fagne is also the fish-filled lakes or "pingos" caused by the creation of stretches of stratified ice beneath the surface of the ground during the last major ice age. As the ice melted, it formed huge circular folds or ramparts, some of them several hundred yards in diameter.

These are not the only natural features in the area. Cotton grass, normally a mountain plant, also flowers occasionally beneath the snow. The drosera is a carnivore. Blueberries and cranberries grow on the drier moorland, as do the fields of heather.

More than 160 species of bird live on the Upper Plateau. We shall mention only one, the symbol of this area - the grouse, which lives, stalks, and breeds here. Unfortunately it is now an endangered species and, after each winter, the number of couples dwindles yet further. There are only some forty left.

Around La Fagne are extensive forests. It's true that the hardwoods are on the decline and that most of the woodland, where pines are now predominant, are partly or totally manmade. Economic necessity leaves little choice.

The largest stretch of woodland is the Hertogenwald (or Duke's Forest) whose history goes back to the days of the Franks and Charlemagne. Its 12,000 hectares of unbroken forest are fairly well-stocked with game.

The Upper Plateau in La Fagne is also of major importance for the country's water supply. Its peat bogs are like huge sponges which give up their huge volume of water in the form of innumerable streams and rivulets. They divide into three basins - Vesdre, Warche and Rur. Around them are a number of lakes (Robertville, Butgenbach) and dams (Gileppe, Eupen).

It goes without saying that all these extensive natural resources had to be protected. Hence the creation of the Hautes Fagnes Nature Reserve (4,200 hectares) which lies with the Hautes Fagnes Eifel Natural Park (67,000 hectares) adjoining Germany's Nordeifel Natural Park and, to the south, the Germano-Luxemburg national park.

A docker at work.

The Fagnes in the snow.

It is also in this region that almost 70,000 German-speaking Belgians live, and German is the third official language (with French and Dutch). Their nine towns make up the "German-speaking community".

The local people had been Prussian since the Treaty of Vienna in 1815, became Belgian again after the Treaty of Versailles signed in 1919, were annexed during the Second World War, and finally became Belgian again after 1945.

These "Eastern communities" (Malmédy must be included in their number) are in some ways Belgium's "Wild East", a sparsely-populated area with vast open spaces well-suited for day trips or for longer holidays. A type of tourism that is activity-based rather than cultural, perfect for the family. And tourism is the region's main source of income. With 300 self-catering flats and villas, 27 campsites, 4 youth hostels, a dozen holiday villages, and more than one hundred hotels, it can cope in any season.

Three itineraries marked with hexagonal signs zigzag their way through the area - the Fagnes and Lake Route, the Our Valley Route and the Castle Route. These circular routes are accessible from any points along their way.

EUPEN is the "capital of the German-speaking community" and the seat of its institutions. Lying at the confluence of the rivers Helle and Vesdre, the old drapers' town has something of the air of a Rhineland village about it and this becomes increasingly marked during certain events such as the **Christmas Market** or the **Rosenmontag Carnival**

The Rose Monday Carnival in Eupen.

Eupen Town Hall.

SKIING

Despite its lack of real mountains (the highest peak stands at 2,255 ft.), Wallonia is an excellent place for cross-country skiing. Above 1,625/1,790 ft. there is sufficient snow for two months or more a year. Nowadays, there are almost 300,000 winter sports enthusiasts in Belgium. The slopes are very popular too with the Dutch, Germans and French from the north of France. Most of the slopes lie in outstandingly beautiful natural settings and the pistes have professional markings. Moreover, the amenities (ski hire, hotels, restaurants) and access (a well-maintained network of roads, the proximity of large towns) are a definite advantage. Most of the slopes are on the Hautes Fagnes Plateau, in the Eastern Districts, and around the Baraque de Fraiture, all of which enjoy the highest altitudes. But there are dozens of other slopes, even in the provinces of Namur and Hainaut. In all, there are 1,240 miles of cross-country tracks spread across 73 "resorts". There are also 11 gentle downhill slopes suitable for beginners and for experienced skiers who want to get back into practice. Sledging, snow scooters (skidoos, skibobs, snowmobiles, and cross-country three-wheelers) complete the range of amenities on offer to sports enthusiasts.

Every year, the "Ardenne & Meuse Tourisme" Association publishes a paper called "Ardenne Ski", a sort of Walloon skiers' bible containing all the necessary practical information. The "Belsud" central booking agency has special offers available for winter sports holidays.

- ARDENNE & MEUSE TOURISME
15 rue de l'Eglise,
6980 La Roche-en-Ardenne
(Tel. 084/41.19.81)

- BELSUD
rue Marché aux Herbes 61
1000 Brussels (Tel. 02/513.86.30)

(Rose Monday). Preparations for this carnival (almost all the region's towns and villages have one) begin in November. The Carnival Prince is enthroned on the Saturday before the event (held on Ash Wednesday) and receives the keys of the city which he keeps until midnight on Shrove Tuesday. The feast day is, then, the Monday during which there is an impressive procession of groups and floats. As elsewhere in the eastern districts, the musical associations play a particularly large part in the festivities.

There is an **upper town** (Town Hall dating from 1665, St. Nicholas' Church built in the German "Hallenkirche" (lit. "hall church") style with Baroque-Rococo decoration, a fountain and Renaissance houses on the Place du Marché, the town's museum, and picturesque streets) and a **lower town** (leading to the dam). Eupen is an excellent starting point for a large number of excursions and trips in the near vicinity, especially in the forest.

The **Vesdre Dam** (or "Talsperre" was opened in 1951. It is 205 ft. high and 1/4-mile long, and stands in a setting of outstanding natural beauty that provides ample opportunity for walking and cycling. There are sailing facilities on part of its 125-hectare lake. From the Observation Tower (107 ft. high, with lift) there is a panoramic view of the lake, the Eupen Forest and the Fagnes (open all year, weekends only in winter).

Another impressive dam, at **La Gileppe** (in Jalhay), was built at the beginning of Leopold II's reign to meet the needs of the wool industry in Verviers, which required pure water. The dam is best-known for the imposing sandstone lion weighing 130 tonnes that stands guard over it. There is an observation point, a

The Vesdre Dam.

The Gileppe Dam.

Water sports on the Butgenbach Lake.

221 ft. tower from which there is a panoramic view, and three walks ($1\frac{1}{2}$, $2\frac{1}{2}$, and 9 miles).

Water is still one of the main characteristics in the tranquil Warche Valley, at Robertville and Butgenbach.

Robertville also has a dam, which holds back the waters of the Warche. But its lake, with its rambling banks bordered by meadows and woodland, plays host to yachts, rowing boats, pedalos, canoes and even motor boats.

In **Butgenbach-Worriken**, a veritable sports holiday complex has grown up around a 120-hectare lake.

A 4-star campsite, 48 comfortably-equipped chalets, and a public sports centre cater for thousands of summer holidayma-

kers or people on courses (outdoor and indoor activities). In the winter, visitors come for the skiing. It is true that the entire region has a well-developed infrastructure encouraged by an average altitude in excess of 1600 ft.

Skiing and water sports are, of course, not the only leisure activities the region has to offer !

Climbers enjoy tackling the **Rocher de la Warche** in Bellevaux-Ligneuville. There are a dozen routes up the rock face to the summit. "High-fliers" indulge in hang-gliding at La Ferme Libert (BéverCé-Malmédy) and the Hautes-Fagnes Flying Club will take visitors on an introductory flight. Riding schools, swimming pools, tennis courts

and crazy golf are legion and every tourist office has its own large-scale ramblers' map. Over the past few years, "Mountain Bike" trips have been organised in Malmédy.

Malmédy, which lies in a dip surrounded by steep wooded hillsides, is first and foremost the town of the "Cwarmê". A Shrovetide carnival prepared over the four previous Thursdays. It is the masked figures who organise everything. The most fearsome are the "Haguètes" who, armed with their "flesh-hooks" (or "happe-tchâr"), catch the necks or calves of by-standers. Many other figures and associations participate in the procession held on the Sunday under the leadership of "Trouv'lê", a sort of Carnival King. Although the Monday is more of a private affair (with short, humourous playlets performed in Walloon retracing the past year's local events), the Tuesday sees the return of the floats and musical associations again and ends with the burning of the Haguète. Russian salad is the standard dish during the carnival, with "Malmédy kisses", a delicious meringue. The taste for festivities and traditions comes to the fore again in Malmédy during the Martinmas ceilidhs and the first Night in May.

The Carnival and Folklore Museum (Maison Cavens) and the Paper Museum (one of the main local industries) are worth a visit. The "cathedral" with its two mighty towers, the Abbey Gardens, the Tanneries Park, a few elegant half-timbered houses and countless shops will no doubt encourage you to stay a little longer. Around the town are several holiday villages.

Malmédy, which is a major touring centre, leads quite naturally to the Hautes-Fagnes Plateau. We have already mentioned its natural resources; it's now time to give you a few more details.

Botrange (the highest peak in Belgium with an observatory and meteorological station on the Signal, alt. 2,255 ft.). The **Nature Centre** (open daily throughout the year, 10 a.m. - 6 p.m.) is really the centre for the Natural Park. The building is an austere affair, built entirely of local materials (quarry stone, wood, and slate). There is an entrance hall with an open fireplace, a shop, an information centre, temporary exhibi-

Top: *The Malmédy carnival.*

Middle: *Botrange Nature Reserve.*

Bottom: *The mossy uplands near Baraque Michel.*

Reinhardstein Castle.

tions, a classroom for environmental studies, an audiovisual display, and a herbalist's shop. It also houses a permanent exhibition showing all aspects of the Fagne's environment. A sort of anti-museum where each theme has its own form and colour, using the most up-to-date techniques (including lasers), and where visitors are encouraged to touch the exhibits. Guided tours available on request. Cycle paths.

Baraque Michel, the Fagne's main tourist centre and the site of a Geodesy Centre. It gets its name from the small inn opened there c. 1812 by a German called

Michael Schmitz. Its bell was often rung to guide lost hikers back to safety in bad weather. Over the years, 126 travellers were saved in this way. In the neighbouring **Fischbach Chapel**, the only service that is still celebrated is the Midnight Mass at Christmas. On **Mont Rigi**, the University of Liège has set up a scientific research establishment. These places form the real heart of the Fagne and are the focal point of any trips on the plateau. Other names will quickly become familiar if you spend some time in the region - Carrefour de Belle-Croix, Colonne Panhaus, Via Mansue-

risca, Croix des Fiancés, Boultè, Noir Flohè, Croix Mockel, etc.

Back on the Malmédy road, it's time to visit the loftiest castle in Belgium set on a spur of rock overlooking the R. Warche, **Burg Reinhardstein**. A path leads up to it from the Robertville Dam (2,600 ft.). The original building dated from 1354 and many famous families owned the castle, including the Metternichs. It has been exceptionally well-restored and furnished, yet Reinhardstein has maintained the austere appearance of fortresses of bygone days. It stands in the midst of 6 hectares of ground.

The R.Our.

The **Our Valley** in the south of the next region on our itinerary is still deep, wild, and untouched by property speculators. Lying at the frontiers of West Germany and the Grand Duchy of Luxemburg, its European vocation is symbolised by the Europe Monument (1977). If you want to discover all the subtle charms of this valley, take the 62-mile long **Ourtal Route.** It passes through **Ouren** which gets its name from the river. One of the two towers on St. Peter's Church has the same shape as a spiked helmet ; then on to **Reuland** with the towering ruins of its 11th-century fortress ; and **Crombach-Rodt** where special measures have been taken to safeguard the environment. The main town on the route is **Saint-Vith**. It has been a bustling shopping centre since the Middle Ages. A monthly market, the St. Catherine Fair, the Martinmas Procession (on the Sunday after the 11th November), the St.Guy Pilgrimage in mid-June, the fête after Corpus Christi, not forgetting the inevitable carnival, all bear witness to its continuing vitality. The 16th-century Büchel Tower is a reminder of its warring history, in stark contrast to the tranquil Wiesenbach Chapel. As for the museum, it has an eloquent model of a traditional local interior. The town has a number of leisure activities to offer visitors, including skittles - a game that is characteristic of the region.

You will come across the R.Our again in **Schönberg** (small lake, modern church, Lourdes-type grotto with a torchlight procession on 15th August) and in **Manderfeld**, an old village much beloved of Charlemagne's family. There are Stations of the Cross dating from 1761 round the Gothic St.Hubert's Church.

Although the Our Valley is not very well known to tourists, it is undoubtedly one of the most picturesque places in the region. Tall forests, vast meadows, windmills, attractive villages, and innumerable tributaries are all to be found along its route. It is never monotonous, often winding, and sometimes downright wild. It is sure to delight walkers and fishermen. In addition to the lakes and rivers, anglers will find ponds and fishing grounds specially designed for their enjoyment.

A brief incursion northwards completes our cursory look at this region. To **Trois Frontières** (Three Frontiers), at the borders of Belgium, the Netherlands and West Germany. There are no less than 28 castles in this area. But they can only be admired from the outside, for they are all pri-

100

vate property. **Raeren** was once an international centre for pottery and stoneware. It was Raeren pottery that Brueghel and so many of his contemporaries depicted in their paintings. The output was exported worldwide. An interesting museum in the feudal castle serves as a reminder of days long gone. Once a manor, **La Calamine** (Kelmis) enjoyed a period of economic prosperity when the estate included the largest zinc mine anywhere in Europe (at Vieille Montagne). The neighbouring community of **Neu-Moresnet** (Gueule Viaduct, 3/4 mile long) still has a typical old town and an impressive wayside cross with 14 carved Stations of the Cross standing in the depths of the countryside. In **Hergenrath**, in the August of odd-numbered years, there is a flower festival during which more than one million flowers are mounted on floats. **Gemmenich** is the gateway to the Dutch Limburg region. **Hombourg** is an extension of the Herve Region which we shall discuss in a later chapter. In **Henri-Chapelle**, the American War Cemetery contains the graves of almost 8,000 soldiers who fell in battle here during the Second World War, and a museum shows the various operations that took place at the time of the Allied Landings.

Through Kettenis, Lontzen, Montzen, Remersdael, Sippenaken, and Walhorn, the environment is lush and green, much gentler than the landscapes in the Fagne. There are countless examples of the country's architectural heritage (farmhouses, castles, and chapels), all of them in an excellent state of repair.

Then there is the obstinately French-speaking **Welkenraedt** with its major cultural and traditional events whose sphere of influence ranges far beyond the limits of the region itself. An attractive floral clock and illuminated fountain is one of only two of its kind in Belgium. There are more than 400 societies and associations in the Trois Frontière region, of which the most characteristic involve the sport of archery where the "target" is at the top of a pole (tir à la perche). The carnival is, of course, one of the usual events and sports amenities abound (sports halls, swimming pools, fishing, crazy golf, footpaths, riding, and tennis).

Countryside in the Our Valley along the "Ourtal Route".

THE HEART OF THE ARDENNE

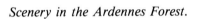

Did you know that the Ardennes have a heart. It beats steadily at all four points of its compass - Bastogne, Houffalize, La Roche, and Vielsalm. And it echoes to the sounds of the dense forests that are still the habitat of large animals. It races on the hillsides, beats breathlessly at La Baraque de Fraiture, and flops down for a rest in the meadows covered with yellow buttercups in May! Deep gorges and gentle clearings, heather and broom, and ubiquitous rivers that beckon you to take a dip and play hide-and-seek with the rocks on the green mountainside. Nature (despite being endangered in some places) is nevertheless the chief organiser everywhere. What more can be said to prove just how suitable the "heart of the Ardennes" is for healthy invigorating holidays ?

Vielsalm is proud of being the garrison town of the Ardennes Light Infantry, the modest heroes of modern warfare (Museum). In the Salm valley, the houses are built of the two local stones - schist and arkose. Yet it is something else that has made it world-famous - whetstone. This shaving stone, although now no longer used, was once exported worldwide. In Salmchâteau, a former workshop has been turned into a museum to bring the stone back

Scenery in the Ardennes Forest.

The Ardennes are an ideal place for cycling holidays, with a wide choice of possible routes.

to life. And the disused industrial site is slowly being taken over by the undergrowth. In the "Thier des Carrières" (nature reserve), there are now 210 varieties of mosses, lichens and ferns covering the slates! With its well-developed tourist amenities (holiday villages and estates in **Golonfa** and **Les Doyards**), Vielsalm has visitors throughout the year, for it is a ski resort in the winter.

In **Mont-le-Soie**, the horse is king (manege, beginners' classes and classes for established riders, treks lasting from two days to a week with cultural activities and tourist attractions).

In "**So Bêchefa**", the forest is not afraid of the human species. On the contrary, it has been ope-

ned up in order to tame him (amenity areas, barbecues, information centres, family walks) and teach him respect!

Blueberries grow in profusion here, and they are used to produce the local beverages. They also form the background to the authentic traditional festivities held on 21st July. On the previous evening, the witches (or "macrâles") hold a colourful sabbath which is much appreciated.

The Petit and Grand Halleux (with the Monti Zoo) provide some of the numerous interesting panoramic views that abound in the Ardennes.

A few miles away is **Beho church**, a fanciful and fantastic building. It contains the Virgin Mary's hair and a remnant of the

Holy Shroud brought back from the Crusades. But it is first and foremost the outside wooden balcony and loggia that astonish visitors. Once they cross the threshold, they are unfailingly amazed at the naive multi-coloured decoration covering the interior.

Gouvy is a large village in the eastern Ourthe. There are 200 miles of way-marked footpaths to keep hikers happy (used for cross-country skiing in winter), while the Cherapont Lake will suit those who prefer beaches or angling.

Typical Ardennes houses (Montleban) mark the start of the climb up to the plateau of Les Tailles and La Baraque de Fraiture. The local equivalents of The Fagnes (though rather smaller)

Cross-country skiing and walking in the Ardennes.

are just as interesting as their counterparts in the east of the country. The plateau towers over the rivers Ourthe, Ourthe Orientale and Salm. It is also the source of two other capricious waterways - the rivers Aisne and Lienne which flow northwards.

La Baraque de Fraiture is one of the crossroads in Ardennes, and one of its highest points (2,120 ft). Downhill and cross-

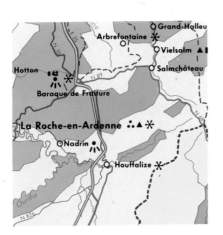

country skiing are popular throughout the sixty or so days in the year when there is sufficient snow. The same is true of Samrée, which takes us down a winding picturesque road to the valley and La Roche.

And this, since last century at least, has been the main tourist attraction in the Ardennes region. In the summer, **La-Roche-en-Ardenne** literally swarms with tourists from all over the world. And why this unfading attraction? A solid infrastructure of hotels and leisure activities, yes, and a certain "je ne sais quoi"... History, legends, crafts, gastronomic specialities, the ideal starting point for many an excursion, La Roche has all that and more. This is indeed "the pearl of the Ardennes". Canoeing, rafting and fishing in the R.Ourthe, cross-country cycling, walks to numerous chapels and the hermitage nearby, hunting grounds, the ruins of a mediaeval castle (at the top of which the ghost of Countess Bertha "really" appears every evening in the summer months), the Deister Forest Park, crazy golf, tennis courts, swimming pool, a small train... And the list could go on. But we have said enough to show that this is a real holiday resort. Local crafts are characterised by the blue earthenware pottery. Sloes are used to make "purnalet", a delightful elixir. A huge bonfire (first Sunday in Lent), a mediaeval banquet, the great mid-Lent Carnival and festivals throughout the summer provide constant local entertainment.

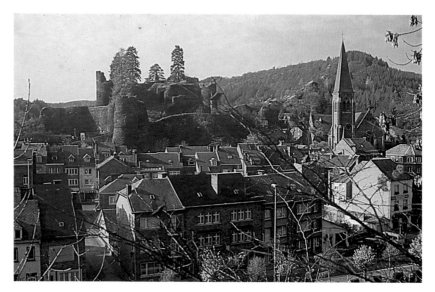

Top : *La Roche-en-Ardennes.*

Middle :
The Ourthe Valley near La Roche.

Bottom :
Canoeing on the R.Ourthe.

Summertime pleasures on the banks of the R.Ourthe.

Halfway between La Roche and Houffalize, take time to enjoy one of the most famous landscapes in Belgium, stretching from **Hérou** to Nadrin. Here, from an "observation platform" at the top of 120 steps, you can see the six meanders with which the mischievous R.Ourthe ensnares the rock. It is a striking sheer cliff face. You would think you really were "in the middle of nowhere"; the environment is totally unspoilt. The fertile imagination of our forefathers even had it that a frightening "black man of Hérou" lived in this spot, but luckily nobody has ever met him... Any number of footpaths lead to the nearby villages of Ollomont (11th-century chapel), Bérimesnil (prehistoric encampment), Mormont, Maboge, Wibrin, Achouffe (Fairy Valley, small-scale brewery), and Artho (mediaeval church).

Close by is the **Nisramont Dam** and its 47-hectare lake (there is an 8-mile long footpath) which provides the drinking water for the entire region. The huge construction is open to the public. **Houffalize** (1268 ft) is a well-equipped tourist centre with accommodation and leisure activities. The multi-purpose Adeps Sports Centre at "Deûs Oûtes" occupies almost 80 hectares of woodland.

In town, the "Panther" (a German tank) is a cruel reminder of the Second World War during which bombing raids wiped Houffalize right off the map. A small local flora and fauna museum bears the name of its patron, Dr. Verheggen. Gastronomic weekends, sports events, traditional entertainments, and other merrymaking over the

The Six Ourthes observation platform.

Christmas and New Year period attract many people to Houffalize. The tombs in St. Catherine's Church are also worth a visit, as is St. Roch's Chapel, the old mills and the fortified farmsteads in the near vicinity. During your walks, you can appreciate how much Houffalize merits its nickname of the "Town of Panoramic Views". Nearby are schist quarry stone houses in the village of Mont and the pleasure castle in Tavigny, one of the most elegant of all Wallonia's villages.

We then go on to **Bastogne**, which has gone down in history as the centre of the terrible Von Rundstedt offensive in the winter of 1944-1945 which marked the start of the Nazis' final retreat. It was during this Battle of the Ardennes that the American General McAuliffe pronounced a resounding "Nuts" to a call for his surrender !

Standing at the crossroads of the Ardennes Region, Bastogne still bears vivid reminders of this bloody episode in its history. The most moving place is undoubtedly the Mardasson Hill and its memorial to the 77,000 American soldiers who laid down their lives during the battle.

Mosaics by Fernand Léger decorate the crypt containing three chapels (Catholic, Protestant and Jewish).

The "Bastogne Historical Center" on the same hill is built in the shape of a five-pointed star. Using some quite exceptional documents, it illustrates "the" battle. It is a living, exemplary museum layout. Everywhere in the town and its vicinity, there are memorials to the terrible winter. A Patton tank and monument, a bust of McAuliffe, tank turrets and one of the "freedom milestones" which line the victorious route taken by American troops

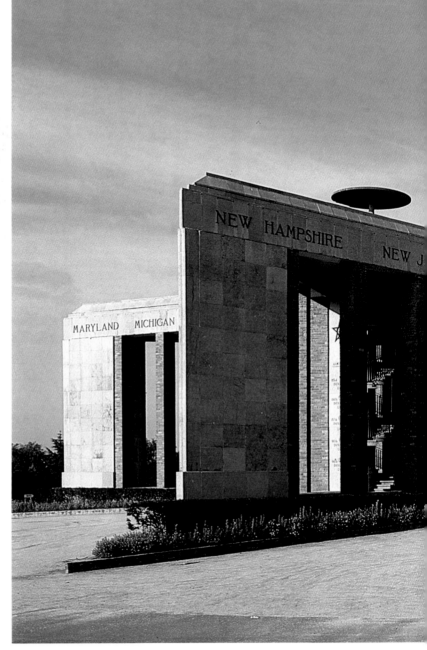

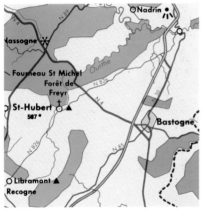

from Normandy down to here.

Because of the constant hustle and bustle (there are 300 shops open every Sunday !), Bastogne was nicknamed "Paris in Ardennes" as far back as the 17th century. So it is not only of interest because of events that took place in the last war. The Trier Gate (Porte de Trèves), for example, with its slit windows and machicolations, is a fine section of the mediaeval walls. And as far as sights worth visiting are concerned, there are the Mathelin Residence and St. Peter's Church.

In December, the Walnut Fair is an opportunity for merryma-

The Bastogne Historical Center.

king and commemmoration. This is the time to taste "Ardennes ham" on which there are strict quality controls. You can follow the main stages in the battle at any time of year by following the signposts, and in the summer a small train takes visitors round. Nearby sights include the church in Rachamps, the German war cemetery in Noville-Recogne, the hillside village of Longchamps, and the ski slopes of Hompré and Senonchamps.

An express road leads to **Libramont** (exhibition centre) where, every year around July 21st, there is the largest agricultural show in the country (more than 100,000 visitors). Among other things, you can watch demonstrations and trials involving the last Ardennes cart horses, which are exported worldwide and which were used by Julius Caesar's legionaries and during Napoleon's Russian campaign.

THE SWEET THINGS OF LIFE

On one side Heinsch, Bonnert, Sterpenich. On the other Chantemelle, Gérouville, and Montauban. Germanic ruggedness; Romanesque delicacy. The names of the towns and villages really are evocative! On one side the Arlon region; on the other, Gaume. Together they make up the Belgian Lorraine, which lies adjacent to France and the Grand Duchy of Luxemburg. And a few miles further on the hills of the Ardennes become winding and more gentle. The three regions have many differences, which they do their utmost to maintain, but they also complement and balance each other out in a very valuable tourist area - South Ardennes and Gaume, Semois and Vierre. Here, as elsewhere in our country, the rivers have their contribution to make! And nature imposes healthy enjoyment in an environment that man has not yet completely tamed.

The region attracts people first and foremost because of the strong character of its people.

There are not many of them. And that's just as well - it leaves more space for everybody else! And they are obstinately and passionately attached to land that is sometimes thankless. Their traditions are long-lasting, their style of cooking is healthy and substantial and their houses make no show of finicky airs and graces.

The area is watched over by four lookouts - Arlon on the eastern front, Virton the advance guard to the south, Neufchâteau the citadel in the north, and Bouillon which surveys the western front. Within these boundaries, the landscapes are attractively varied. They range from the deep green of the Anlier Forest (the largest hardwood forest in Belgium) to the bright yellow ochre of the Jurassic Gaume area. And everywhere, there is the sparkling R. Semois, a capricious

bit of water if ever there was. For example, it wanders over 80 miles between Tintigny and Rochehaut instead of taking the direct route 26 miles long. It's true, though, that nothing ever runs in a straight line here!

This is a place where history is never told in dazzling accounts of times past. Yet history is more ancient here than anywhere else. Arlon shares with Tongres and Tournai the title of Oldest Town in Belgium. The Celts settled in Virton, and the castle in Bouillon is the best-preserved reminder of mediaeval architecture anywhere in the area, no less!

If you wanted get the true feel of this region, you would have to cross it on foot so that you could listen to its heartbeat and appreciate its often very subtle nuances. The local tourist offices outshine each other in their enthusiasm and ingenuity when it comes to marking out some quite astonishing walks. And there are thousands of miles of footpaths. Long-distance waymarked paths, some of them. The vast 125-mile long ''Holiday Gaume'' circular route ('Gaume buissonière'') has been laid out starting from Aubange. And anybody who completes the entire length in a week, which is not bad going, is entitled to a medal!

The R. Semois.

Two Gallo-Roman sculptures in Arlon's Luxemburg Museum.

This is a land of hikers, and a land of fishermen. The Semois, Vire, Ton, Rulles, Vierre, and Mellier are all well-stocked rivers. **Arlon** has been the province's main town since Belgium gained its independence. It owes its importance to a key geographical situation which placed it at the crossroads of the routes from Rheims to Trier and Tongres to Metz as far back as Roman times.

The **Luxemburg Museum** has a collection of 425 Gallo-Roman sculptures, which makes it the largest of its kind in Belgium and one of the foremost in Europe. The **Roman Tower** (and its underground museum) and the **archaeological park** (hypocaust, old graveyard, 1st-century baths, and the ruins of a Christian basilica) are places of quite outstanding originality.

These days, Arlon has all the charm of a bustling small provincial town. It climbs up the southern slope, or "knipchen", of a range of high hills at the top of which is **St. Donat's Church** (observation platform with panoramic view of four countries - Belgium, Grand Duchy of Luxemburg, Germany and France). The entire district underwent very successful restoration a few years ago. In the remainder of the town there are squares, open spaces lined with official buildings, wide avenues, and countless shops, all providing a sense of movement and vitality.

Just like the Mid-Lent Carnival or the traditional Lent broad beans (in February), not forgetting the Maitrank festivities during two weekends in May. The **maitrank** (literally, the Maytime drink) consists of white wine used to macerate woodruff picked before it flowers. A little sugar, some brandy, a drop of champagne and it's ready to serve - chilled !

Without wishing to commit perjury, it is a well-known fact that the Semois rises in Arlon.

A few miles from Arlon (which is also a garrison town with numerous sports centres) lies Autelbas where you can visit the ruins of Clairefontaine Abbey (13th century), and the mausoleum of its founder, Countess Ermesinde of Luxemburg.

The **Arlon Region** is as varied as anyone could wish for, with the mineral deposits in Halanzy, the sand and heath of Stockem, the wooded moorland of Arlon, the Anlier Forest, and the slate quarries of Martelange. There are also the astonishing landscapes of the Upper Sûre Valley which forms

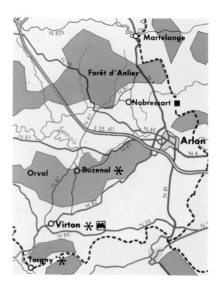

the extension to "Luxemburg's Little Switzerland" in the **Martelange** area where tourist amenities have been well developped. A walk in the Anlier Forest (picnic and barbecue areas) is worthwhile for the sight of fine robust farmsteads that are typical of the area.

In **Habay-la-Neuve**, at the other side of the forest, the lakes and castle of Le Pont d'Oye are a must for visitors, and they are as romantic as you could wish for. In the 18th century, the Marchioness of Le Pont d'Oye led an adventure-packed existence which is still talked about to this day. Among other things, she was "Master of the Forge", which serves as a reminder of the importance of the iron industry in Gaume two centuries ago. Every year on the last Sunday in September, Habay holds an event in honour of the forest and organises a friendly meeting of bards.

The **Gaume Region** is the Belgian Riviera, its Provence, you might say ! A region protected from chill northerlies by the southern slopes of the Ardennes. A region that enjoys a veritable microclimate - and that's no tall story ! If it was, how could there be 3,000 vines in Torgny (a lovely village with red tiled roofs) which, since 1956, has been producing the refreshing "Clos de la Zolette" that is reminiscent of Riesling !

In Gaume (386 sq. miles, pop. 85,000) some municipal buildings are still called town halls - in **Virton**, for example, at the confluence of the rivers Vire and Ton that gave the town its name. And the tiny capital of Gaume is proud of its title. The people here are jovial, friendly, perhaps a little bit critical of the powers-that-be. And with a marked sense of humour, they hold the "Lovers' Fair" every Boxing Day. Another fair, but an economic event this time, is held in Ethe at the begin-

ning of August, and there is an important European Film Festival in November, all proof of the area's vitality. The local people are proud of their past but they also live the present to the full. Archaeological digs have been going on in the region for decades now and have brought to light a number of very valuable remains.

Some of them are on show in the **Gaume Museum**. The unusual feature of this museum is its five sections in five different places scattered around the outskirts of Virton - Gallo-Roman pottery in Houombois, Rural Life in Montquintin, Local History in Latour (the famous Dragoons !), an archaeological park in Buzenol-

Montauban (in the midst of a protected area with the reproduction of the famous "Treveris' grain harvester" described by Pliny the Elder). And, of course, the Virton Regional Museum in the outhouses of what was once the Recollects Convent, a first-class representation of the history of all the facets of the Gaume region.

Yesterday and today, we said. The **Rabais Valley** on the edge of Virton has been used as a 80-hectare tourist area that fits in well with the environment. There is a multipurpose hall, lakes, a 4-star campsite, and two holiday villages. An ideal spot for activity-packed holidays. And its success has been proved by its

Virton Museum.

visitors from many different countries.

But the "professional holiday-makers" of the year 2000 do not live in a confined universe. They move around and demand new sights and experiences. In Gaume, they can see tiny villages with attractive names such as Sainte-Marie-du-Semois, Vance, Châtillon, Dampicourt, or Fratin, where communal fountains and washhouses still exist. Strange villages indeed with small squat houses nestling close to each other in villages full of streets but almost devoid of squares. With a few hamlets here and there but very few isolated buildings.

Tourists can go and dream in the "Fairy Hole", gaze in astonishment at the Gomery dolmen, and check whether the remains of the "barbican" at Neuve-Forge/Saint-Léger really do belong to the Four Aymon Boys.

In the summer, never a weekend goes by without some event full of village joviality enjoyed by visitors who are made very welcome if they want to join in the merrymaking.

At the end of the winter, the custom of the winter bonfire is celebrated with much gusto (Old Father Winter is burnt, along with the evil spirits).

Here as elsewhere in the beautiful province, the houses are bedecked with flowers. Partly to welcome visitors, it's true, but also out of respect for the inhabitants themselves and for their houses. A wide-ranging annual competition bears a very appropriate name, "Luxemburg, A Clean Province full of Flowers".

Tintigny (best-known for its cabinetmakers) appears to be the centre of this region. After skirting round it to the north and crossing the R. Semois at the place where it is joined by the R. Rulles, head northwards to Neufchâteau, taking a detour round

The transept in the former Orval Abbey church.

one of the ski slopes.

Neufchâteau is a small town at the junction of roads from Ardennes (which we are in at present) and the Grand Duchy of Luxemburg. The Griffon Tower

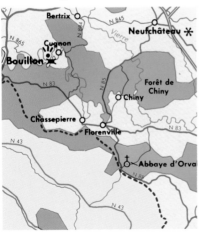

dates from mediaeval times. Although the old districts in the town are rather more recent, they are still very attractive. From the top, there is a picturesque view of the Vierre Valley and the Herbeumont Forest. Angling, boating, indoor and outdoor sports are all commonplace here. July is a musical month and in August the Gauls return, to the accompaniment of some joyous merrymaking ! The surrounding area is full of places to visit. If you have your camera, make sure you have plenty of spare film because you'll be tempted to use it again and again. In Ebly, Longlier, Hamipré, Straimont or Martilly, we are on land that once belonged to the thousand-year-old county of

Chiny. The Counts reigned (and the word is used advisedly) over 57 castles and 1412 villages ! Their coat-of-arms still adorns the arches of the St. Nicholas Bridge. Chiny, which is a summer resort, is well-known for a sports centre that attracts top-class athletes. It is also the starting point for a quite exceptional excursion - a trip down the R.Semois in flat-bottomed punts catering for 10 - 12 passengers at a time. As the boats pass beneath the double-arched Paradise Rock, they cross a fall of rock that is worthy of a canyon before reaching **Lacuisine**, so named because the place was used as a kitchen when the Counts were hunting. The trip lasts one hour and visitors return to Chiny either by bus or on foot along a 3-mile path.

Not far from Lacuisine lies the little-known **Epioux** estate (the castle was used by Pierre Bonaparte when he was in exile).

On the estate, which is a nature reserve, angling is permitted on the five lakes fed by numerous rivers and streams. Let's say it once and for all - water is omnipresent, rippling, accessible, navigable, and warm enough for swimming in the summer. The bridges are not too large to be human and they inspire many an amateur artist. Manorhouses, justice crosses, forges, and low squat houses inevitably catch the eye of walkers in an area that is a hikers' paradise.

Pastoral and scenic romanticism is visible whichever way you

The chapter house in the former Orval Abbey.

Orval, the old cloisters overlooked by the new minster.

The R.Semois in Florenville.

The Semois Valley.

turn. In **Martué**, for example, where the R.Semois carves out what is almost a peninsula ; in the flower-decked community of **Izel** which consists of two hamlets, Pin and Moyen. At this point in our trip through the forest, showing the appropriate amount of serenity, we come close to **Orval Abbey** which was founded in the 11th century by one of the Counts of Chiny. The Cistercian monks had considerable power, which they exercised over some sixty farmsteads and 7,000 hectares of land and ironworks. The Abbey

was destroyed during the French Revolution, rebuilt by the Trappists and consecrated in 1948. You can still imagine how it once looked as you wander through the mediaeval ruins that stand adjacent to the modern buildings resplendent in their warm austerity. The medicinal herb garden and pharmacy and the crypts (housing a Museum of Monastic Life) are open to the public. And whatever your beliefs, you must attend one of the simple yet solemn church services. Finally, no visit to Orval would be complete without the

purchase of bread, cheese, and the beer that is one of only six real Trappist beers brewed anywhere in the world.

The R.Semois then disappears from view until you reach the other side of **Florenville**, a large village at the borders of the Ardennes and the Gaume region, just a stone's throw away from the French frontier. Its reputation as a holiday resort dates from long before the last war. And seasonal entertainments abound. If walking tires you, ''Caroline'' will save your energy. ''Caroline'' is a minitrain that runs along four different lines in the near vicinity. And did you know that Florenville is famous for its flat potatoes said by gourmets to have their own very special taste?

We have now arrived in **Chassepierre** and have found the R.Semois again, which we shall continue to follow from now on. A veritable gem of rural architecture that is full of character and attracts dozens of artists and craftsmen to the largest market of its kind anywhere in Belgium, held every year on the first Sunday after August 15th. Be sure to visit outstanding natural features and historical sights in the area, such as the dolmen in Azy Woods, the Fairy Hole grotto in Chauffour, the Stone Age cave, and the wayside cross that links it to Laiche.

Once you get to **Sainte-Cécile**, you are really in Ardennes. And what will you visit first? The views from the Castellaon Rock, the Mill, or the Knights' Grave, or at the 3/4-mile long tunnel on a disused railway line? On the right bank is Cat's Rock with its panoramic view, then Conques and its priory (once a retreat for the monks of Orval), its viaduct towering some 130 ft. above the R.Semois, and finally **Herbeumont**, a beautiful village with steeply-sloping streets. The cordial, permanent and vitally-important Semois becomes more capricious from this point on, playing at to-meander-or-not-to-meander around the remains of the fortress (the river was well protected!). It then joins forces with the rivers Cugnon and Dohan in long meanders that are almost oxbow lakes. The gentle waterway has suddenly become spirited and impetuous... It is said to have been in **Cugnon** that the St. Remacle, the evangelist of the Ardennes, had his hermitage. It is a long pleasant walk up to the hermitage now, with, at the end, one of the two or three dozen beauty spots along the Semois' course that are "worth a detour". Back in the village, there is a 18th-century castle, old shale houses, Gallic ramparts and a slate-roofed mill. From **Dohan** (castle-farm dating from the 17th century, the Hayon Residence that is now a listed building), you can go on to "Witches' Leap", the Roche Percée (Pierced Rock) or Noir Fontaine (Black Fountain) (the forest setting of the "hideous mill") - on horseback if you like. Pony trekking is one of the region's organised leisure activities.

And here we are in **Bouillon**, one of the absolute "must's" for any visitor to Belgium. There is a splendid panoramic view of it from the observation platform (161 steps) in the village of Curfoz. But that's the subject of a different chapter!

BETWEEN THE RIVERS SEMOIS AND LESSE

From Bouillon, the R.Semois "climbs" up the Ardennes and takes all the time in the world to reach the top. This is tobacco land - and Resistance country. Elsewhere, it is the more rustic, tumbling, clear waters of the R.Lesse that are in the limelight. The Famenne Depression takes us to the edge of the gently-rolling Condroz, then returns close to the dark line of the Ardennes forests. And everywhere, nature is king.

The "impregnable" fortress in **Bouillon** was besieged 17 times over the course of the centuries. These days, it is the tourists that give the assault every year! In order to avoid the castle and its promontory, the R.Semois flows in a loop. Godefroy, the most famous of all the Dukes of Bouillon, sold his castle to the Prince-Bishop of Liège in 1095 so that he could take part in the crusades. He was elected "King" after the capture of Jerusalem. The castle is one of the finest remnants of mediaeval architecture anywhere in the Western world - it has towers, drawbridge, guardroom, thick walls, torture chamber and dungeons. Successive modifications have done nothing to alter the personality of this extraordinary building. In the former Governor's Residence, the Ducal Museum on the hillside houses a presentation of local life and history. A small train will take you round the town and the neighbouring hills. Experienced hikers, who are sure to enjoy themselves here, know that the Ardennes-Eifel long-distance way-marked footpath passes through this spot.

When the R.Semois leaves Bouillon, it becomes lazy, turning and meandering continually to take in some incomparable, monumental natural features - the **Giant's Tomb**, for example, (Le Tombeau du Géant) in Botassart where the river has worn a passage for itself through the hard schist. The view stretches into a luxurious green infinity, as it does

Bouillon, encircled by the R.Semois.

The fortress in Bouillon.

in "The Pulpit" (La Chaire à Prêcher) in Poupehan, close to Corbion, where the poet Verlaine spent long periods of his tumultuous existence. Not forgetting Cordemois Abbey, maintained by French Cistercian nuns since 1935, from which you can see the "Gallow's Rock" (Rocher des Pendus).

Rochehaut (highly appropriate - it means "high rock" !) is an arts

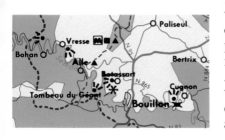

and crafts centre. Large numbers of holidaymakers come on courses here year after year. An exhibition hall can be used for any type of craftwork. From here, there is a view of the small holiday resort of **Frahan** with its squat houses huddling round the church. Visitors are always struck by the obvious majesty of the place.

Alle on the left bank of the river was a major slate centre before becoming the "capital" of Belgium's tobacco industry. It was a former primary school teacher who, in 1855, was the first person to try growing a variety related to the "Kentucky". Although tobacco-growing was a very lucrative business for many decades, it is now no more than a secondary occupation and is slo-

119

The last remaining tobacco crops
are a rare sight. Here, tobacco
in Vresse.

Tobacco cutter in Vresse Museum. ▷

wing dying out altogether. Yet the
tobacco drying sheds have not
disappeared from the region's
landscapes, even if they are used
more and more frequently to
store farm machinery, when they
are not being used to garage
(excessive numbers of) caravans.
The Récréalle Centre is just the
right size for tourist leisure
activities.

In **Sugny**, another typical village, people will still tell you emo-
tional stories of the terrifying witches' sabbaths and of how many
of the participants ended up at the
stake after witchcraft trials. **Mou-**

zaive (slate roofs, pedestrian bridge), **Laforêt** (Old Forge Museum, fountains and drinking trough, bridge of trays used to carry the tobacco and cereal harvest from one bank to the other), **Chairière** (fine church with Passion reredos, leisure centre), **Gros-Fays** and **Petit-Fays** (drystone farmsteads) - these are just some of the places on the Resistance Route whose 57 miles bear constant reminders of the dogged and sometimes bloody, but never useless, fights put up by those who belonged to the Resistance Movement at the risk of losing their own lives. Crosses, chapels, and entrenchments amongst the forest greenery are reminders of their exploits.

Vresse sums up the region's aims and attractions through its tourist and cultural centre. The Tobacco Museum is surrounded by major works by great landscape artists(Marie Howet,Albert Raty, Camille Barthélemy) from the Vresse and Semois School. The St.Lambert stone bridge spans a tributary of the Semois. It has played host to thousands upon thousands of easels...

Another tourist centre is **Membre**, part of the rich Bohan National Park. The "Jambon" (Ham) beauty spot, the Eight Semois Walk (where the river winds its way through the hills in a series of eight turns), the Saloru Rock, and the Fairy Table standing stone can all be seen along the way.

And what is left ? **Bohan** (and its Sugary Kiss cakes - baisers sucrés), the first (or last) Belgian village on the banks of a river which, in French, is written Semoy. A gem of "Namur's Little Switzerland". A reputation that is almost entirely justified. The spring is still celebrated by the lighting of fires of young wood. There are 25 waymarked footpaths around the large village which was once also a centre for the peaceful art of smuggling alcohol and tobacco.

And so we continue across the Orchimont Plateau and **Nafraiture**, in a clearing in the depths of the forest (church with modern Stations of the Cross), and here we leave the river once and for all. But in a country that was born from water, you're never "dry" for long. Beyond Gedinne, the R.Houille stretches into the distance !

The upper plateaux become few and far between, there are fewer villages, and the Louettes (St.Peter and St.Denis) stand guard over **Gedinne**, a large characteristic village (church with an oak reredos, arboretum, ski slopes at La Croix-Scaille).

Until the 19th century, Vonêche was a major centre of crystal glass. And further on, **Beauraing** became known to Christians

The Château de Lavaux-Sainte-Anne.

The Han-sur-Lesse cave.

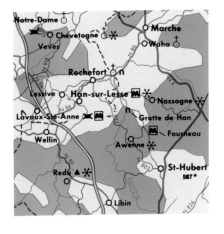

throughout the world because of frequent appearances by the Virgin Mary (1932-1933). It is now a place of pilgrimage (with a Museum dedicated to the Virgin Mary). After Pondrôme, we reach the R.Wimbe and go on to **Lavaux-Sainte-Anne** which stands isolated in the Lesse Valley. The mediaeval castle standing in the midst of a moat and flanked by towers houses a Hunting Museum. And its outhouses praise the "intelligence of the peasant-stock", a disagreeable phrase if ever there was one! Every summer the Lavaux Games bring a theatrical dimension to the traditional "son et lumière". Now let's pay homage briefly to the "Unusual Landscape Route" (Route des Paysages Insolites) as we pass Ave and Aufee, and **Belvaux** that is well-known to potholers. It is here, in the Belvaux swallowhole, that the R.Lesse disappears underground, only to re-appear 18 hours and several miles later in the cave at **Han-sur-Lesse**. This cave, which has undergone exploration since 1777, is one of the finest anywhere. You reach it by railcar (soon to be replaced by a more "revolutionary" mode of transport) from the village centre (Subterranean World Museum). It is a gigantic place and visitors are shown only a third of it. The 420 foot high Dome Chamber is the most impressive section. But the Trophy Chamber, the Styx Gallery, and a boat trip complete with cannon fire so that visitors can hear the echo, ensure that the visit is spectacular. It would be a pity not to see the neighbouring wild animal reserve in the heart of the Lesse and Lomme National Park. Visitors drive through it in a safari-car so that they can see most of the European mammals, some of which have disappeared from our own areas.

Strangely enough, old and new almost rub shoulders with each other at this point. The history of

The Satellite Telecommunications Station in Lessive.

Han goes back millions of years, while **Lessive** turns resolutely towards the future with its satellite telecommunications station (interesting visit) and the dish aerials in the midst of the countryside, all directed towards the satellites.

In **Wanlin,** the "skassîs" (stilt-walkers) ford the river as part of the Whitsun celebrations. And the Belgian royal family spends its holidays in Ciergnon and Villers-sur-Lesse.

Chevetogne is doubly interesting. The Valéry Cousin provin-

THE CAVES

Underground Wallonia is a veritable geological treasure trove. It conceals subterranean riches (grottos, caves, and swallowholes) in numbers that are quite out of proportion to its surface area.

Caves, as you know, are produced by the slow wearing away of limestone rock by rivers filled with carbon dioxide from the air. The slightly acid water infiltrates any cracks in the rock and widens them gradually, forming chambers and galleries over hundreds of thousands of years. Because they fire the imagination and are cloaked in mystery, caves have always been a source of fascina-

tion to visitors. In Wallonia, the first ones were opened to the public at the end of last century. It goes without saying that dozens of them are only accessible to potholers. After all, theirs is a fragile beauty and pollution (much of it manmade) is an ever-present danger. This means that they have to be preserved and the National Committee for the Protection of Underground Areas of Outstanding Natural Interest (Commission Nationale de Protection des Sites Spéléologiques) plays a major role in this work.

The best-known cave of all is the GROTTE DE HAN formed by the R.Lesse. With the caves in

Rochefort and Hotton (discovered as late as 1958), it forms an exceptionnal triangle cutting through the great strip of limestone that runs between the Ardennes and the Famenne depression.

You can take the longest underground boat trip in Europe on the Rubicon which flows through the Remouchamps cave. Goyet has grottos and caves, as have Couvin and Petigny. Dinant has two caves open to the public. There are more in Ramioul, Comblain-au-Pont, Floreffe, and Hastière.

For further information, contact : AGECID,
rue Notre Dame 3, 5000 Namur.
Tel.no. 081/71.20.16

cial estate, a transition area between the Condroz and the Famenne, jealously protects its 500 hectares of natural environment. But it also provides every possible type of sports and leisure facility for families who might like to stay on the luxurious camp and caravan site, unless they prefer the authentic foresters'house.

A Benedictine monastery and an oriental (Byzantine) church stand adjacent to the Estate. They were requested by Pope Pius XI with a view to bringing closer together the churches of West and East. This is the largest church of its kind in a non-orthodox country and the little piece of oriental piety set in the green countryside of Wallonia is very lavishly decorated.

Rochefort (the "Capital of Laughter" because of the major international French-speaking festival, held in spring) is a major tourist resort. It is very much

"alive"! You can visit caves hollowed out by the R.Lomme, and although they are less spectacular than the ones in Han, they are more rugged. Close by, the chapel of Notre-Dame de Lorette is an exact copy of the one in Loretto (Italy). Pierre Bonaparte, Lafayette and Chateaubriand all stayed here. In the summer, a mere flight of fancy will take you to the nearby beauty spots of Doan, Lavaux, and Lessive. And, of course, no visit to Rochefort would be complete without tasting the authentic Trappist beer made by the Cistercians of Saint-Remy (open to male visitors only, on request).

The main fact that lingers in your mind about **Marche**, the largest town in Famenne, is that it is one of the very few industrial centres in Belgian Luxemburg but crafts have not disappeared altogether; they are represented today by lace-making. The Tourelle (the

remains of the mediaeval town walls) has been turned into a regional museum. In **Waha**, the remarkable little Romanesque church contains the oldest consecration stone anywhere (1050). Marche is a place where people tend to live well and its speciality is "matoufé" (a mixture of flour, milk, bacon and eggs). It is also famous for its 1900's Bird Market, which takes place on 15th August.

The town is a major road junction and it takes us quickly on to the Ardennes Forest, which is still untouched. A "Forest Route" runs through the vast stretch of woodland that so worried Julius Caesar! A pleasant place for nature-lovers, game-hunters, and skiers (the hills here are high). **Nassogne**'s collegiate church houses a sarcophagus containing the bones and vestments of St.Monon which are carried in procession on the Sunday after

The open-air Wallonia Country Life Museum.